Telling Tails

From Hopeless Hounds to Tyrannical Tortoises — Animal Letters to

The Telegraph

EDITED BY
IAIN HOLLINGSHEAD

CARTOONS BY MATT

Aurum
Press

Quarto is the authority on a wide range of topics.

Quarto educates, entertains and enriches the lives of
our readers—enthusiasts and lovers of hands-on living.

www.QuartoKnows.com

First published 2016 by
Aurum Press Ltd
74–77 White Lion Street
London N1 9PF
www.quartoknows.co.uk

A catalogue record for this book is available from the British Library.

ISBN 978 1 78131 592 7
eISBN 978 1 78131 659 7

10 9 8 7 6 5 4 3 2 1
2020 2019 2018 2017 2016

Typeset in Mrs Eaves by SX Composing DTP, Rayleigh, Essex

Printed and bound in Great Britain by CPI Group (UK) Ltd, Croydon, CR0 4YY

'Well, this is awkward . . .'

SIR — If you feed a cat it thinks it is God; if you read the *Guardian* you think you are intelligent; if you've got any sense you read the *Telegraph* and keep a dog.

Jonathan Goodall
Bath

SIR — Where do you turn if you have no dog? S.J. Perelman had a fix for this concern: 'Outside of a dog, a book is a man's best friend.' To which he puckishly added: 'Inside of a dog, it's too dark to read.'

Dick Laurie
London SW15

CONTENTS

INTRODUCTION

Of all the popular topics which attract weighty postbags to the letters desk of *The Daily Telegraph* (the defence of the realm; the storyline in *The Archers*; the best way to locate a missing spouse in a large supermarket), few are as much fun as the readers' witty observations on the animal kingdom. We are fortunate that *Telegraph* letter-writers don't just share their lives with their pets; they are also more than happy to share the eccentricities of their pets' lives with the rest of us – whether that be a Newfoundland with a talent for salmon fishing; a cat addicted to *Ski Sunday*; a sheep who thinks it's a dog; or a tortoise with a penchant for head-butting.

The readers are similarly acute observers of nature beyond the kitchen doors. To paraphrase Monty Python, their interest includes the short, the squat and the venomous, from migrating midges to foaming toads, as well as the bright and the beautiful, from love-sick peacocks on village greens to albatrosses in the merchant navy to nightingales accompanying the opera in Holland Park.

It has, therefore, been a huge pleasure to mine the archives, like a chaffinch in search of the juiciest worms, to uncover the best letters of the past decade or so. Here you will find: the final word on pigeon's regional accents, as well as donkeys who will only answer to a Lancastrian brogue; a dog who paid his vet in golf balls, as well as a crow who stole everyone else's; a cat and a horse decorated by the military for bravery, as well as an anti-terrorist St Bernard who fell asleep on operations; an MP who rode to Parliament on horseback, as well as a rural pub-goer who lurches home the same way. Along the way you will also encounter guest appearances from Lord Byron's dog, Baroness Thatcher's cat and an army major who soothed over a diplomatic incident by giving Idi Amin a coveted pair of white peafowls.

Most of all, however, you will find a love and respect for man's best friends in all their guises, feathered, hooved and/or tailed, all equally bewitching, beguiling and bewildering. I hope you enjoy spending time with Tutankhamun the Tortoise and Percy the Peacock as much as I have.

Iain Hollingshead
London SE22

MY FAMILY AND OTHER ANIMALS

FAMILY PECKING ORDER

SIR – I was fascinated at the tantrums displayed by Prince Henrik, Denmark's Prince Consort, on learning he had dropped from 'number two' in his family hierarchy. I know the feeling – having three children I was always number five until, one evening, I arrived home from an arduous day to find two golden retriever puppies in the kitchen, and my wife greeting me with: 'I'll just get the dogs' supper and then I'll see to you.'

From five to seven in seconds, with nowhere to go.

Ronald Best
Eastbourne, East Sussex

SIR – I sympathise with Ronald Best. Some years ago I managed to get an earlier flight back from a business trip. As I came through the door my wife looked up from the dinner table and asked: 'What are you doing here?'

My four children continued their meal. The dog was genuinely pleased to see me. The next day I went out and bought a second dog. After that I was always assured of two good welcomes when I came home.

Martin Hughes
Bracknell, Berkshire

SIR — I enjoy visiting my local florist, who often says: 'Hello, handsome' when I enter her shop, but I suspect her greeting is directed at my dog rather than at me.

Ian Burton
Boxmoor, Hertfordshire

SIR — You report that 'mothers-in-law languish behind pet dogs in the family popularity stakes'. An infallible test to ascertain which of the two loves you more is to lock them both in the boot of your car for a couple of hours, and see which one is more pleased to see you when you let them out.

John Mash
Cobham, Surrey

SIR — We have two sons, a dog, a cat and 15 tortoises. Where does that leave me?

Paul Mason
Long Sutton, Lincolnshire

THE TOADS MORE TRAVELLED

SIR — Taking pets on holiday is nothing new. In the 1960s my father would load the following into his Humber Super Snipe: mother, four children, one dog, one tortoise, one budgie, several guinea pigs, two goldfish, some stick insects and, on one occasion, a ferret.

He would deposit us at our holiday home and then, very sensibly, return home to seek the sanctuary of his bank in the City before collecting us at the end of the holiday.

Alexis Granger
Bracknell, Berkshire

SIR — Your correspondent is uncertain as to how to behave when driving behind a 'Baby on board' sticker.

I faced the same dilemma recently when following a 'Ferrets on board' sign on a car near Skipton, North Yorkshire.

Dr Ann Chippindale
Oxford

SIR — I was watch-keeping officer on the bridge of a ship outward-bound from Greenhithe to Goole in the 1960s, with one helmsman (whose chief purpose was to give me someone to talk to about the fleshpots of Goole), when a Dutch coaster passed us inward-bound.

The only occupant of its bridge was a dog, with its paws on the dodger, smiling as only mongrels can smile. As it could obviously identify port and starboard buoys and knew the rule of the road, I flashed it a message with the Aldis lamp, but it declined to reply.

Ian Dougall
Bournemouth, Hampshire

SIR — The Bichon Frise dog flown as baggage on Concorde is not the only supersonic animal. Our domestic tabby cat, Harriet, broke the sound barrier on June 19, 1998. A fault in the heated hold of our scheduled jumbo led BA to offer the cat an upgrade.

Her certificate has pride of place in our loo.

Clark McGinn
Harrow-on-the-Hill, Middlesex

SIR — In 2011 it causes merriment if a man tries to board a train with a pony. This would not have been remarkable 100 years ago.

Selina Hastings's biography of Nancy Mitford recounts that in the summer of 1911 the family moved to High Wycombe. They went by train — four children, their parents, three dogs and Brownie the pony.

When told the pony was not welcome in the guard's van, 'Farve [their father] changed their first-class tickets for third, and they all, including Brownie, travelled in the same compartment.'

Dr Matthew Down
Jesmond, Newcastle upon Tyne

SIR — Passengers boarding or alighting from trains with their horses at Crewe will have no difficulties because the 'horse landing stage' still exists, across from platform 12.

However, these days it seems mostly to be used for bus rail replacement services.

Roger Croston
Christleton, Cheshire

SIR – While not condoning the Chinese tourists who kept an undeclared rabbit in a hotel shower, I have taken my house rabbit on holiday with me on many occasions.

She has a 4ft by 2ft 6in cage and is happy to take walks on a harness and lead (she has been vaccinated against myxomatosis and HVD). She does not demand constant attention, has no tendency to wander off hunting, does not rush up to lick passersby, and she is silent, with no yapping or barking.

I would consider her a much more desirable guest than a dog or cat.

Diana Elsdon
New Malden, Surrey

SIR – Diana Elsdon takes her rabbit to hotels. In Kuala Lumpur, we once used the bathroom of our room in the Hilton as temporary accommodation for our well-travelled Amazon parrot.

He seemed perfectly happy there, although we had to apologise to the staff for his appalling language.

Richard Evans
Evercreech, Somerset

PARROT PRANKSTERS

SIR – I used to own an African grey parrot called Charlie. His favourite trick was to peer from his position in the sitting room to the bottom of the garden and, when he saw our Jack Russell dog reach the very end of the garden, he would whistle loudly, in the manner in which I whistled the dog.

The perplexed hound, abandoning its reason for running into the garden, would turn around and return to the house thinking it had been hailed.

Charlie would then emit the wheezy laugh which Mutley used when taunting Dick Dastardly.

Roy Williams
Aberporth, Cardiganshire

SIR – Joey, my grandmother's African grey parrot, lived through the Second World War in a basement in Barnes, in south-west London.

In later years, one of Joey's tricks was to imitate the sound of a cluster of falling bombs: a series of descending whistles. On hearing this, her Airedale would dive under the table and stand there shaking, its tail between its legs. The parrot would then imitate a man's uproarious laugh.

Allen Chubb
Haslemere, Surrey

SIR – I was having brunch with the former owners at Amberley Castle, when a phone rang in the next room. No one moved.

'Oh, it's only the parrot,' they said. 'He'll stop ringing in a minute, then he'll answer the phone and have a conversation.'

Moira G. Maidment
West Clandon, Surrey

SIR – I've just returned from a few days in a hotel in Mombasa where a very talented parrot whistles excerpts from Colonel Bogey and *The Good, the Bad and the Ugly*, as well as some wonderful wolf whistles.

Of course, being a Swahili-speaking parrot, he also greets his visitors with a resounding *Jambo*.

He gets a due mention on TripAdvisor.

Chris Hayman
Sowerby Bridge, West Yorkshire

SIR — A few weeks ago I checked out a hotel in Llangollen in north Wales. It had good reviews, with many customers mentioning the resident parrot in the reception area. But scrolling down the comments, I saw that one disgruntled client had posted a report complaining that the parrot had sworn at him as he was leaving.

Surely a good reason to visit.

Michael Cattell
Mollington, Cheshire

SIR — I once saw a small advertisement in a newspaper that read: 'For sale. African Grey parrot. Would suit retired victualler or deaf clergyman.'

David Chapman
Worcester

SIR — I used to go into a pub in Marton, North Yorkshire, where the barman, Jack, kept behind the bar a myna bird that he taught to speak. Every time a customer ordered a drink, the bird said: 'And one for Jack.'

Needless to say, Jack never bought a drink.

Peter Gilbert
Thames Ditton, Surrey

SIR – Some years ago I was visited by a parrot, an African Grey called Henry.

'Can you talk?' I asked Henry.

The bird cocked its head, gave the matter some thought, and replied loudly: 'No.'

Tim Deane
Tisbury, Wiltshire

BUTLER VS BUDGIE

SIR – It was not only at meal times that Churchill's budgie, Toby, left his mark, as you report.

This much-loved creature slept in a special cage in Churchill's bedroom during his peace-time premiership in the 1950s. The cage was opened when ministers gathered for matutinal confabulations before the great man got up.

In his diary, Churchill's private secretary, Anthony Montague Browne, gives an affectionate account of Toby 'flying round the room, pecking at Cabinet papers, taking nips from the whisky and soda at the Prime Minister's bedside and settling upon the domed head of the Chancellor of the Exchequer with the inevitable consequences'.

Rab Butler, the Conservative politician, came to these meetings with a special silk handkerchief which he used to mop up after Toby, murmuring: 'The things I do for England.'

From his master Toby received only kisses, never rebukes.

Lord Lexden
London SW1

MAD DOGS AND THEIR ENGLISHMEN

SIR – As a regular visitor to Britain, I have been intrigued by the recent spate of letters regarding the television-viewing habits of readers' assorted pets. These have reinforced my view that the British are quite, quite mad. Long may it be so.

John Eagle
Adelaide, Australia

SIR – Our late cat, called Bismarck, was a great fan of *Ski Sunday*, watching the proceedings religiously every week.

Our dog was a devotee of opera, and once howled himself hoarse during a documentary about the life of Maria Callas.

Mary and David Halbert
Kingsbury, Warwickshire

SIR – My cat Pushkin was fascinated by snooker on television and would dive under the set to see where the potted balls had gone.

Danni Phillips
Slough, Berkshire

SIR – Our late collie enjoyed sport – in particular golf and rugby – but hated cartoon animals and DIY adverts and would bite the television whenever these appeared.

Once, while golf was showing on the kitchen television, he got in the way of cooking, so my husband took him into the living room, where he watched it for the rest of the afternoon. He would always try to catch the ball just before it was struck.

Philomena Smart
Ewell, Surrey

SIR – My Border collie's favourite television programme was *Strictly Come Dancing*. He was fascinated by the close-ups of steps being made by the dancers.

Tony Wheatley
Chichester, West Sussex

SIR – Our dog Alfi slept soundly through the epic tennis match between Federer and Stakhovsky. No sooner had the match ended than his reveries were rudely terminated by the noise emanating from the highlights of Sharapova vs De Brito.

He rose with a start from his slumbers, anxiously looking around, trying to locate the pair of humans who were so obviously enduring the most excruciating pain.

Richard Childs
Chichester, West Sussex

SIR – Yes, mumbling actors are very annoying, but could I make a plea to restrict the use of the distant, barking dogs so often used to create atmosphere in drama? All this does is arouse my dog from his sleep on the sofa, setting off a spate of barking which makes it even more difficult to understand the actors.

James Logan
Portstewart, Co Londonderry

SIR – In the evening, when I settle down to watch television, my pet rabbit sits on my knee and promptly falls asleep. More often than not I join her.

Frank Hanson
York

DOG DAYS OF DECEMBER

SIR – Well, I have seen it all now – Advent calendars for dogs.

Presumably it is thought that they'll understand the meaning of Advent when eating their treats each day.

Cynthia Crocker
Devizes, Wiltshire

SIR – My friend, who keeps her horse, Champ, at my house, bought him an equine advent calendar last year. Dutifully, I pinned it up outside his stable, well out of reach.

At 3am I awoke to a noise. I went outside to investigate and discovered my horse, John Wayne, had let himself out of his stable and was busy helping himself to the treats in the advent calendar. In my nightie, in the dark and rain, I picked up horse treats assisted by Trevor, the dog.

At least this seemingly useless present kept three of us entertained, albeit at an untimely hour.

Stella Baylis
Welland, Worcestershire

SIR — We were relieved that we had not been subjected to any 'round robins', but now find ourselves on the receiving end of several cards from our dog-obsessed friends that have been 'signed' by their child substitutes. This must stop.

Robin Welland-Jones
Oakhanger, Hampshire

SIR — Some friends of ours send cards from their dogs to other dogs. If that wasn't bad enough, the cards are edible.

John Smith
Great Moulton, Norfolk

SIR — One festive offering I always await with dread is the annual swipe at the Christmas newsletter.

Not all of us spend our year locked into social media sites, nor do we all have friends and family in close proximity.

I say bring on the dog's health, the grandchildren's activities, the holidays and hobbies — and humbug to the cynics.

Barry Carter
Oxford

SIR — You report the story of a woman who is spending £2,000 on her dogs at Christmas. My poor Nova Scotia Tollers will have to make do with a four-mile walk, a swim in the lake, mud up to their elbows, a few squirrels to chase, my left-over sprouts and gravy on their evening meal, then a sleep by the fire. Lucky they don't read the paper.

Nairn Lawson
Portbury, Somerset

SIR — Further to your report of Marks & Spencer refusing to send a greetings message to a man called Dick, a friend of mine received flowers via the M&S service and the card read: 'With love from Steve, Kerry and the cat (name too rude to print).'

The cat's name was Puss.

John G. Randall
Wigan, Lancashire

SIR — To date my cat hasn't received any Christmas cards, but last week he received a letter from his vet congratulating him on using a particular flea treatment.

I'm now worried that my charming post lady will think that my real name is Wonky Wilkinson.

Frank Wilkinson
Bolton, Lancashire

SIR – Frank Wilkinson's cat should count itself fortunate to receive from the vet a letter only about flea treatment. Our border terrier, named Dyson, received a letter from his vet beginning: 'Dear Dyson…'

The gist of the letter was that, now he was all of six months old, he would be much happier without his testicles. It invited him to ask his owners to make an appointment.

John Ward
Great Bookham, Surrey

THE VET WILL SEE YOU NOW

SIR – When one of my horses sustains a leg injury, my vet asks to see the animal in motion before any treatment is suggested.

I have a knee injury. I have seen two doctors, three physiotherapists and a knee specialist. Other than entering and leaving their consulting rooms, not one of them has asked to see me in motion. Three months later I am in the same condition.

Maybe I should consult my vet.

Tim Stafford Thornton
Morpeth, Northumberland

SIR – Tim Stafford Thornton should certainly try his luck at the vet. A friend of mine, tired of getting no treatment from her GP, took her dog's anti-inflammatory medication and was playing tennis a few days later.

Kate Graeme-Cook
Tarrant Launceston, Dorset

SIR – My GP recently prescribed me some ear drops at the same time as a vet prescribed some for our dog. Whether it was due to my wife losing her glasses, I know not, but I got the dog's and the dog got mine. It didn't seem to do me any harm.

Christopher Cox
Warnham, West Sussex

SIR – My neighbour's West Highland terrier has been prescribed a course of tablets by her vet. The instructions read: 'May cause drowsiness. If affected, do not drive or operate machinery. Avoid alcoholic drink.'

Joyce Bonnelt
Crowborough, East Sussex

SIR – During their advance through Europe in the Second World War, leaders of 45 Commando, in which my father, Hugh, served, preferred the help of local vets to doctors in the event that one of the men was wounded or fell ill. They took the view that if a vet was capable of curing an animal that couldn't tell him where it hurt, there would be no misunderstandings arising from the language barrier.

It is recorded that this practice saved the lives and limbs of many servicemen.

Richard Muir
Gerrards Cross, Buckinghamshire

SIR – The enthusiasm recently displayed by your correspondents for consulting a vet instead of a doctor would, I fear, soon wane upon the first requirement for a temperature reading.

John Benson
Harpenden, Hertfordshire

LAMB AGA SAGA

SIR — Your report on the sheep that thinks it is a dog after being brought up with three puppies provided much amusement for my family.

We have a four-week-old Castlemilk Moorit orphan lamb happily sharing the garden by day, and the Aga by night, with three whippets, a retriever and a large lurcher. Recently, this canine majority was further increased when our two children arrived for lunch with their two terriers and two Rhodesian ridgebacks.

In spite of being outnumbered, the lamb continued to rule the pack.

Nigel Thursby
Patney, Wiltshire

SIR — We had a lamb that was orphaned at three days old; we had no option but to bring it inside, and bottle-feed it.

It soon thought that it was one of our sheepdogs, playing football with them outside. It was initially known as 'lamb, lamb' but before too long became known as 'that damn lamb', especially as it used to rush upstairs and jump on our bed, waking us up.

Candy Haley
Cobham, Surrey

THINGS THAT GO BUMP
IN THE NIGHT

SIR — As a young vet some years ago, I was presented with an aged Yorkshire terrier by owners of a similar age. They were concerned the dog was becoming vicious.

It seemed the dog was sleeping in their bed, and when they moved in the night the dog bit their toes, waking them up.

They ignored my obvious advice. I examined the dog's teeth. It didn't have any. I advised them they were in no danger of serious injury.

They departed somewhat dissatisfied. I waived my fee.

Roger Westhead
Cheddleton, Staffordshire

SIR — Since my husband died, my Tibetan spaniel has been upgraded to Gentleman of the Bed Chamber. A very satisfactory arrangement for both.

Joanna Butterwick
Pinkneys Green, Berkshire

SIR – During my impoverished days, I found that a Jack Russell, tucked in about an hour or so before I retired, warmed the bed as efficiently as an electric blanket and (pro rata) at considerably less cost.

After she had performed such a valuable service, it seemed unkind to remove her.

June Green
Henley-on-Thames, Oxfordshire

SIR – Thelma and Louise share our bed every night, with their accessories: my husband's discarded socks, a soggy tennis ball and a plastic pheasant.

In spring, Jasper the cat joins them, occasionally accompanied by a wild rabbit he has hunted down and dragged through the cat flap in the early hours.

Lynn Moss
West Hatch, Somerset

SIR — Each morning our cat comes to share some quality time in bed with us while we read *The Daily Telegraph*.

Having pounced on the bed, he invariably heads for the front page to make himself comfortable. Any attempt to relocate him is met with fierce resistance.

On the odd occasion he will make do with the business pages — but he never accepts the sports section.

John Lane
Burseldon, Hampshire

SIR — One of my great pleasures in life is daydreaming in a warm, scented bath with my Burmese cat purring contentedly on the edge while my loyal spaniel sits on a stool keeping a drowsy, watchful eye over me.

Sometimes I ask my wife to join us.

James Logan
Portstewart, Co Londonderry

BOADICEA'S NAME SHAME

SIR – What has happened to the good old dogs' names? Where are the Pals, Rexes, Laddies, Butches and Rovers? In the past month, while walking our two beagles, we have met Randolph and Watson, both beagles, Moriarty the Irish red setter, Boadicea the Irish wolfhound and several others.

Some of these animals look positively embarrassed when called by their owners.

Jim Hamer
Bolton, Lancashire

SIR – My son, who lives near Cape Town, has a black Labrador called Taxi. I always feel foolish standing on a remote beach trying to get her attention.

Paul Sugden
Ramsbury, Wiltshire

SIR – I had a friend whose father was a Methodist minister, and they had a black cat called Satan. We were always amused to think of him calling the cat in at night.

Bronwen Hawks
Billingshurst, West Sussex

SIR — Some years ago I lived next door to a young couple who kept the wife's horse in a stable at the bottom of the garden. Eventually a stray cat gave birth to one kitten, which she decided to keep.

'I'm going to call it Jesus because it was born in a stable,' she told me.

She changed her mind when I pointed out to her the inadvisability of standing at the door late at night shouting: 'Jesus! Jesus!'

Rosalind Hellewell
Scunthorpe, Lincolnshire

SIR — My French wife and I had a wonderful little cocker spaniel called Ollie.

This was not a problem until we got to France, where my wife was looked at somewhat sideways as she wandered about shouting 'Au lit!'

Vincent Hearne
Nabinaud, Charente, France

SIR – My father and I wanted another Sealyham terrier and my long-suffering mother did not. The dog duly arrived and we called it 'Quits'.

Quits lived a long and happy life, looked after mainly, of course, by Mother.

Liz Beaumont
London SW1

SIR – I am reminded of the gentleman whose wife was able to reply truthfully to demanding phone calls by saying that her husband was 'away on Business', when he was enjoying a day on his hunter of that name.

Marjorie Stratton
Chippenham, Wiltshire

SIR – I knew a doctor who named his dog after a dictatorial clinical director, so that he could have the pleasure of shouting: 'Sit! Stay! Down P---!'

Dr Graham Read
Wigan, Lancashire

SIR — A friend's son called his new puppy Achilles, purely for the pleasure of hearing his mother shouting 'Achilles — heel!' while walking on Hampstead Heath.

Jane Cullinan
Padstow, Cornwall

SIR — When I lived in a suburban, semidetached house as a boy, my father named our ginger tom Perkins. Asked why, he said: 'When we call him from the garden at night, people will think we have a butler.'

Canon Rodney Matthews
London E4

SIR — When I was at school in London, there was a caretaker named Mr Fido, who had a dog called Bosun. All hell broke loose when we got them the wrong way round.

Iris Marriott
Liskeard, Cornwall

SIR – Some years ago, a friend of mine owned a dachshund that was called Nimrod. One day, the dog was knocked down by a car and lost a leg. He was renamed Tripod.

Peter Robinson
Marlow, Buckinghamshire

SIR – I have suspected for a good few years that the name Max for dogs has been growing in popularity, as you report. While strolling in local parkland with my wife, I have often attempted to respond to what I assumed were distant greetings from enthusiastic acquaintances, only to find some slavering hound rush heedlessly past me towards the source of the cry.

I really must look at re-branding myself.

Max Craven
Derby

SIR – Peter Ustinov had an amusing story of walking his aunt's dog in the Cheltenham area.

Whenever he called the dog, some door would open and an elderly gentleman would ask: 'Did someone call?'

The dog's name was Major.

Capt W.H. Eggert
Poringland, Norfolk

SIR — Bulwark, Albion and Corunna were the evocative names of our three wonderful Labradors.

Bulwark was my favourite ship, Albion my last ship, and Corunna my most beautiful ship.

Lt Cdr Michael Brotherton (retd)
Chippenham, Wiltshire

SIR — Alexander Pope's epigram on the collar of a dog belonging to the Prince of Wales read: 'I am His Highness' dog at Kew; Pray tell me, sir, whose dog are you?'

Su Sainsbury
Sunbury on Thames, Middlesex

SIR — Byron not only gave a suitable name, Boatswain, to his Newfoundland (a breed that loves water), but also wrote a deservedly celebrated epitaph for the creature:

'Near this spot are deposited the Remains of one who possessed Beauty without Vanity, Strength without Insolence, Courage without Ferocity, and all the Virtues of Man without his Vices. This Praise, which would be unmeaning Flattery if inscribed over Human Ashes, is but a just tribute to the Memory of Boatswan.'

Penelope Lowder
Northampton

SIR – My daughter had a cat called Ceremony. When visitors called she would say: 'Come in, don't stand on Ceremony.'

Maggie Pogmore
Downham Market, Norfolk

SIR – We once had a cat called Magnifi, a ram called Battering, and a gander called Mahatma.

Steve Schroeter
Auckland, New Zealand

SIR – We acquired a young, male rescue cat. He has long hair that he is blithely uninterested in grooming; in feline terms, his colouring is 'blue'; and he is highly intelligent and great fun to be with.
We named him Boris.

S. J. MacDonald
Ilford, Essex

SIR – We named our pedigree Tonkinese cats Polly and Esther, as they are a manmade breed.

Jenny Cobb
Five Ashes, Kent

SIR – T.S. Eliot wrote that all cats have three names. The first is the one the family are allowed to use. The second is his particular name, the one he uses when he wants to seem dignified. The third is his 'deep and inscrutable singular Name', which he never reveals to anyone.

Val Lewis
Shepperton, Middlesex

SIR – The naming of cats, according to Old Possum (T.S. Eliot), is a difficult matter. He goes on to cite examples, such as Admetus, Electra, Demeter, Munkustrap, Quaxo, Coriscopat, Bombalorina, Jellylorum – 'all of them sensible, everyday names'.

Who are we to argue with the great poet?

Leslie Frizell
Hove, East Sussex

SIR – About half a century ago, the *New Statesman* ran a competition inviting readers to specify which 'human' names were least likely to be given to a cat. The winners, as I recall, were Alan and Keith.

Graham Healey
Sheffield

SIR — Thomas Hardy's infamous dog 'Wessex' was aptly named, but I wonder how Hardy's cat felt about being called 'Kiddleywinkempoops'.

Diana Goetz
Donhead St Mary, Wiltshire

SIR — Cats should have short names that will stand the test of being shouted out repeatedly at dead of night. This is why I call mine Tycho.

My tortoises, who do not need short names since they never come when called, are Clytaemnestra and Aristophanes.

Arthur Ord-Hume
Guildford, Surrey

SIR — Is there something in the psyche of tortoise owners, or is it the influence these creatures have on their owners, which urges us to give them heroic names? As a child, my tortoises were called Tutankhamun and Cassiopeia, although they, too, never came when I called.

Caroline Horsley
Cogolin, Var, France

SIR — My tortoise is called Walnut; she does come when called.

Annie Garnett
Shaftesbury, Dorset

TASTY TREATS FOR TOASTIE THE TORTOISE

SIR — Recently I have had visited upon me a small Moroccan tortoise by a lovely granddaughter whose interest in animals has now turned to kittens.

However, we are struggling to find food it will accept: Toastie (the tortoise) will eat nothing but anemone leaves.

I have gone about gathering the most juicy of dandelions, from which he always retreats as if they were poison.

I have also tried nasturtiums, marigolds and other edible flower leaves, to no avail.

In desperation I obtained a 'total holistic dietary food of dandelion flavour', but when offered it he closed one eye before turning away as if to say, 'You must be joking.'

My once-proud anemones have been reduced to a row of bare stalks.

I would value any advice from readers.

Ray Smart
Bottesford, Leicestershire

SIR — Many years ago we had a tortoise that ate snails. She held down the shell with one forefoot, pushed her head into the opening, and hauled out the occupant. Unfortunately this useful trait was offset by her penchant for young lettuces.

Elizabeth Champion
Salisbury, Wiltshire

SIR — Our friend's tortoise comes to the back door and knocks on it until it is opened and fruit or vegetables offered. He especially likes apples.

David J. Hartshorn
Badby, Northamptonshire

SIR — Timmy, our tortoise, would stick his head into half a tomato and munch on a lettuce leaf or two, but would only finish off with a Jacob's Cream Cracker. Ordinary supermarket crackers were left untouched.

Malcolm McCoskery
Buckhurst Hill, Essex

SIR — In 1982 I inherited a spur-thighed tortoise with a basement garden flat that I bought near Holland Park in London.

'Ferdi' turned out to be an energetic, rather bad-tempered tortoise with a penchant for escaping. When we moved to a terraced house in Ealing he would often squeeze through a neighbour's fence and be found marching down the road, his shell covered with Able labels bearing our address.

When we moved to rural Worcestershire, he roamed around a well-fortified pen in our garden, and would inevitably make a run for it if we were distracted when we let him out to graze the lawn.

A motorist once found him on the main road to Worcester and foisted him on an unsuspecting family for a month before we retrieved him.

After 27 years of loving care, he finally left us one summer's day by perfecting the art of pole-vaulting over his wooden fence while we were out.

I do not miss the restlessness, the headbutting attacks or the intolerance he had for our pet dogs and cats, but I admired his determination to escape year after year. I hope he roams the woods and farmland for as long as he wishes.

Catriona Craig
Malvern, Worcestershire

SIR — The nation's sympathy will have gone out to the owners of Timothy, the 160-year-old tortoise whose death was reported this week. However, his longevity pales into insignificance by comparison with Cardinal Wolsey's tortoise which — according to the late Professor E.L.G. Stones, the distinguished medievalist — was killed by a petrol-driven lawnmower in the grounds of Hampton Court Palace, allegedly at an age of at least 350.

James Gray
London SW1

THE SCHOOL NATURE RUN

SIR — Clive Aslet argues that rural children are at a disadvantage compared with their city counterparts. I've lived in a village in Hampshire since I was five. We have a friendly pub, numerous tractors steaming up and down our country lanes and a group of friends of my age within walking or cycling distance.

My little sisters, who are nine and 11, spend their time pedalling up lanes. If they're not cycling, they're collecting conkers, blackberries, and dandelion leaves for the many guinea pigs which my sister has bred, and which sometimes range free underneath the apple trees. Or they're catching crayfish in the chalk streams and boating in the old sandpit bottom.

If this sounds idyllic, it is. We have a tame pheasant called Archibaldson, and two crazy dogs. Our school run is like a nature trail, with herds of deer, boxing hares, tiny leverets, a large barn owl and different birds of prey. And no traffic. Sometimes we do stop, but only to chase dozy partridges out of the way of the car.

True, at 13 I'm not as streetwise as my London cousins, but public transport isn't rocket science, and it isn't the 15th century where I would have to travel to the nearest city by cart.

As for being a bunch of country bumpkins with no social skills, cultural understanding or confidence, we have plenty to say for ourselves, and some of us even read the papers.

Am I bored? I'm a teenager — boredom is what I do best.

Iona Todd
Stockbridge, Hampshire

BROAD SHEETS

SIR – Your correspondent tells us that *The Daily Telegraph* fits the windscreen of his car to prevent frost. It is also a precise fit as a lining to our rabbit hutch, and highly absorbent, too. *The Times* used to be on standby until they shrank it.

Martin Duhig
Tonbridge, Kent

SIR – I give my used *Telegraph*s to a hedgehog sanctuary to be used as bedding.

Apparently they are far superior to other newspapers for this purpose.

Ros Fitton
Solihull, Warwickshire

SIR – My teenage cat enjoys my stillness while viewing the television, but objects to my reading *The Daily Telegraph* because of the disturbance caused by turning the pages. Readers may be pleased to note that he has taken well to the Kindle edition.

Dr Peter Stuart-Smith
Ombersley, Worcestershire

SIR — Why do you continue to use ridiculously glamorous models on your fashion pages, demoralising the average reader?

My own, somewhat more dishevelled, Airedale is still scrutinising the photographs in today's paper, looking for evidence of old dinners in the beard, which we all know to be the mark of a real dog.

Val Russell
Blackburn, Lancashire

'Just fetch the newspaper.
Spare me the moralising'

LIFE OUTSIDE
THE DOG HOUSE

HOW TO TELL IF YOUR DOG IS A TORY

SIR — Our dog Ben has savaged all electioneering material pushed through our letterbox, with the exception of any communication from the Conservative party. My son even tried reposting the same flyer, but still no mauling from Ben.

Are we to conclude that our dog swings to the right?

Sally Hudson
Tilehurst, Berkshire

SIR — My father stood as a Conservative Parliamentary Candidate in Bilston in the 1950 general election.

One of his favourite stories involved knocking on a door after a day of campaigning to be greeted by an elderly lady who promised that she would definitely vote for him.

When asked why she replied: 'You have a Bulldog and I love Bulldogs.'

Jonathan E. Godrich
Clee St Margaret, Shropshire

SIR – I am becoming increasingly offended by references to Tony Blair as a 'poodle'. I have a black standard poodle called Toto. He is a big, strong dog: proud, brave and intelligent.

Could you please desist from this slander?

Noel Aspill
Stamford, Lincolnshire

HALT! SITZ! BLEIB!

SIR – In late 1945 my father, who was a farmer, was stationed in Vienna, where he rescued a starving, beautifully trained army German Shepherd. The animal was aptly named Loot and smuggled back to Britain.

Unfortunately, Loot never learnt to respond to commands in English, and shouting to the dog in German in rural Berkshire in the late Forties was fraught with risk.

Loot lived until the mid-Fifties, and apparently remained grateful for having been rescued.

Nick Pope
Woodcote, Oxfordshire

SIR — The dog that only answers to a French accent reminded me of when we fetched our donkeys and, at first, they ignored our greetings, despite having been friendly to their previous owners.

We soon remembered the owners hailed from Blackpool. Once a cheery Lancastrian cadence had been adopted ('June! Come here, lass!'), all was well.

The donkeys have since tuned in to received pronunciation.

Rosy Drohan
Bath, Somerset

SIR — I am very pleased to learn that Latin and Greek GCSE vocabularies are to be reduced. My dogs have a vocabulary of more than 30 words. Soon a Latin GCSE will be within their grasp. Could this be the origin of the term 'Dog Latin'?

Jane Mynors
Petworth, West Sussex

SIR — Following the unbelievable news that pupils who have suffered recent bereavement of their pets will get extra marks, might we expect that, one day, pupil's pets may even be allowed to take their exams for them? Owners of dolphins and collies will obviously have a considerable advantage.

David Mansfield
London EC2

A HUSBAND'S BEST FRIEND

SIR – I was sorry to read that Rod Stewart's marriage at 45 to a young lady of 21 was not a success. My first wife and I parted company amicably after some 30 years. I remarried at 59, a young lady of 23. I am now 87 and have spent the happiest days of my life with my present wife.

The secret of our harmony has been dogs, particularly long-haired dachshunds. As I am patron of the Longhaired Dachshund Club and a life member of the Canine Defence League, whose logo is 'A dog is for life', it may be surmised that this influence of the canine in human affairs is splendidly beneficial.

Sir James Walker, Bt
Port Soderick, Isle of Man

SIR – I once arranged to meet a man for a blind date in a cosy rural pub that turned out to be the finishing point for a dog-walking event. We shared our table with a Labrador, a Jack Russell and a springer spaniel.

The result was a relaxed, amusing and fun first date, greatly enhanced by the dogs and their chatty owners. My companion and I married three years later and always greatly enjoy answering the question of how we met.

Anna Figiel
Hindhead, Surrey

SIR — You report that Major General Cowan believes people should not sit next to their spouse at dinner. Finding myself next to my wife at a dinner party I found it necessary to discuss the dog's flatulence in the absence of the hound who was completely innocent at home.

Paul Atkins
St Albans, Hertfordshire

SIR — None of the men in Jane Fonda's life were 'capable of intimacy', you report. What Jane Fonda needs to understand is that when a woman needs emotional support she turns to another woman. However, when a man needs emotional support he turns to his dog.

Jonathan Goodall
Bath

SIR — Several friends have recently got dogs. Not because they are female and they feel safer with one, but because they are male. Without a dog, a man walking alone is regarded with suspicion — with a dog a man is considered normal, not avoided and even spoken to.

Veronica Bliss
Winchester, Hants

SIR – I was glad to read that one in 10 people prefers dogs to humans. Now it has been confirmed I am not alone.

My dog does not ask my age, does not care if I indulge in a whisky after our morning walk or scowl if I put on my PJs by 7pm. He also sleeps on my bed, but does not hog the duvet – love you, Buster.

Ellie Green
Charvil, Berkshire

SIR – I resent being told that, as a dog owner, I look like my pets. We have a brown Labrador and a Jack Russell. I do not resemble either of them. I look like an Alsatian.

Jeremy Woolcock
Great Bardfield, Essex

URBAN HUNTING WITH DOGS

SIR – I recently let our spaniel out into the garden to chase away an urban fox. I have been agonising over my legal position ever since. Was I hunting with a dog, or using reasonable force to protect my property?

Anthony Gardner
London NW1

SIR – A few evenings ago our terrier started barking excitedly at the front door. Having put him on a lead, I opened the door, to be greeted by the sight of a fox fleeing down the front steps and into the road.

Like a water-skier, I was towed along in pursuit by the dog, with the fox calmly maintaining a 10-yard safety zone. At this point, the chairman of our local tennis club rounded the corner with his terrier, also on a lead. Now sandwiched between two dogs, both straining on their leads, the fox disappeared into the tennis club grounds.

This raises a number of questions in light of the proposed legislation. First, if our two dogs had not been on leads, would the chairman and I have been liable for a £5,000 fine each for allowing our dogs to hunt as a pack?

Second, as chairman of the tennis club, would my friend have been liable for a further fine for allowing a dog to hunt across the club grounds?

Finally, as the freeholder of the tennis club, where would the London Borough of Lambeth have stood in all of this?

Nicholas Holliday
London SW2

SIR – Once I handle my dog's lead, he jumps and spins around in excitement. His brain is not telling him he is going for walkies to a coffee house in Islington: it is telling him, 'We are going hunting'. When he sniffs the air, it is not for the aroma of the coffee, but: 'Is that a squirrel I smell, or a rabbit? Or a cat? Let's hunt it down, chase it and kill it.'

All dogs are hunting in their minds.

Alan Taylor
Cookham, Berkshire

SIR — We live overlooking a stretch of the river Tweed, where an incident occurred in the 18th century which resulted in a landmark court ruling.

The Earl of Home, when fishing for salmon, would be accompanied by his Newfoundland dog, which could apparently catch 20 fish in a single morning. The neighbouring landowner was so incensed that he took the dog to court for illegally depleting salmon stocks.

The Scottish Court of Sessions was convened to hear the case of 'The Earl of Tankerville versus a Dog, the property of the Earl of Home'.

Judgment was given in favour of the dog, it being decided that it had not acted through malicious criminal intent but by natural instinct.

Canon Alan Hughes
Wark, Northumberland

SIR — Your report of the golden retriever catching a trout brought back memories of our golden retriever. He would stand patiently on the edge of a friend's goldfish pond, lifting water snails from the water and gently depositing them on the bank. When they were put back in the water he would emit a huge sigh and start the process all over again. He never broke a shell or damaged them in any way.

B.J. Booth
Devizes, Wiltshire

SIR — While I was exercising my whippets in Hyde Park, we headed for an open space north of the Serpentine. After I let the dogs off the lead, they spotted a squirrel, chased and almost caught it, whereupon I was approached by three policemen and told that this was totally unacceptable, to put the dogs on leads and that, if it happened again, I would be reported.

Within a minute, and before I could catch the dogs, one had caught and killed a squirrel. The patrol car returned and the dogs and I had our details taken. I received a summons to appear before Bow Street magistrates. I pleaded guilty, in writing, to disturbing the wildlife in the park and await my punishment.

Rosemary Brooks
London SW3

SIR — I once rescued a squirrel from my dog. The dog suffered a lacerated tongue and I had perforated fingers requiring tetanus injections. The squirrel, unharmed, continued on its way to the tree from where it calmly observed the blood and multiple carnage below.

Jack Burkitt
Digby, Lincolnshire

POSTMAN BITES BACK

SIR — It was interesting to read your report that 'After 100 years, Labrador is top dog'. As a much-bitten ex-postman of nearly 15 years' standing and an unwilling expert on dogs, I would beg to disagree.

There are two distinct types of Labrador: the archetypal, sloppy and loving version referred to in your report; and a second, vicious, biting, barking variety, identical in appearance to the first.

These horrible dogs, as aggressive as pit bull terriers at their worst, are the result of the ridiculous pedigree system so coveted by the Kennel Club and unscrupulous breeders. Bred in Labrador, in-bred in England: approach strange Labradors at your peril.

R.G. Mack
Cheriton, Hampshire

TELLING TAILS

SIR – Further to the recent 'Labradors versus postmen' correspondence, as a young postman I was bitten regularly by a fierce Labrador misnamed Amity.

I married her owner, and the dog never bit me again, nor did she ever attack a postman. Meter readers, water-board men and the occasional burglar, yes – but never a postman.

The solution seems obvious.

Kenneth McAlpine
London SE10

SIR – The answer to the problem of dangerous dogs is the Velo-Dog revolver, invented by the Frenchman Charles-François Galand, to deter dogs in pursuit of one's bicycle.

Unfortunately revolvers have been banned by the Government so that, like dangerous dogs, they are available only to criminals.

Neil Beeby
Machynlleth, Montgomeryshire

NO DOG IN THIS FIGHT

SIR – To separate fighting dogs, each owner should stand behind his pet, take hold of the rear legs, lift them off the ground and walk slowly backwards. The dog cannot reach round to snap at the human holding his back end, and once the threat has been removed from his face, he will calm down very quickly.

If you are alone, then choose the dog which is winning, or is bigger, or is not yours, and take hold of that one.

The method works every time, but only on dogs. Lions, giraffes and elephants require other stratagems.

Len Marshall
Stamford, Lincolnshire

SIR – Len Marshall has obviously never tried to separate two berserk Jack Russell terriers. Once they have sunk their teeth into each other's throats, you will find each with a mouth full of torn flesh if you do manage to tear them apart – and then you will probably have to extract your testicles from the dog left furiously dangling in your hands.

With Jack Russells, it is best to wait until they have their death grip, then two of you grab each around the neck with both hands and try to separate.

If you are alone, a bucket of cold water and loud prayers are sometimes efficacious.

Kim Wallsworth
Wotter, Devon

SIR — Soda syphon. Works a treat.

Robert Parker
Ashburton, Devon

NO DOGS DOWN
THE DOG AND DUCK

SIR — Recently we stayed at a country pub in Wales where we were warmly welcomed. When they realised we had a Labrador in the car, they asked if we'd like to sleep with our dog (certainly not) or if we wanted to eat with our dog (not particularly).

Our dog was then invited into the bar for some quality time with the other dogs. But, to our horror, he blotted his copybook by peeing against an oak post. This resulted in his immediate repatriation to the car for the rest of the evening and night.

I am not surprised that some people find their dogs are not always welcome in pubs and shops. We run a bed and breakfast and welcome dogs with their owners, but the 'ground rules' list is getting longer.

Carolyn Chesshire
Leintwardine, Herefordshire

SIR – All animals that lick their bottoms should be kept out of restaurants – and houses, for that matter.

In my teaching days as a biologist, I used to say that dogs which enthusiastically lick the faces of their owners are merely using the human face as a convenient handkerchief.

Geoff Milburn
Glossop, Derbyshire

SIR – I don't know about dogs in restaurants, but I can't understand why they are not admitted (on a lead) to public buildings, such as shopping malls and office blocks.

My dog is certainly much more spruce than many humans that I see hanging around.

Margaret Bridger
London SE24

SIR — Recently in St Omer en route to the ferry we politely asked (as always) if our well-mannered doberman could enter a restaurant. The charming manager said that our dog was far more welcome than the crowd of horribly ill-mannered (English) children who were running riot while their parents simply ignored them.

Anne Cotterill
Thrapston, Northamptonshire

SIR — On a visit to Spain, I heard an Englishwoman remonstrating with a Spaniard who had maltreated his dog. 'Madam, in Spain, we may maltreat our animals,' he replied. 'In England, you maltreat your children.'

Ken Williams
Blackfield, Hampshire

SIR — Ban dogs in pubs? Your correspondent should avoid living in France.

At a good restaurant recently, a couple at the next table ate a grand meal of oysters and lobster, watched by their little yorkie dog. When finished, the waiter cleared the table and brought a plate of finely sliced cooked ham, which the wife fed, slice by slice, to the dog on her lap.

Until we made our position clear, guests even turned up at our dinner parties with their dogs.

David George
Grimaud, France

SIR – Dining with an American friend in a French restaurant some years ago, my friend asked the waiter for 'un doggy bag'.

Looking puzzled, the waiter went away and came back at the end of the meal – with a bag of bones for the dog.

Margarete Isherwood
Leamington Spa, Warwickshire

SIR – Over-zealous staff are not always responsible for the removal of lone diners' unfinished meals, as your correspondent suggests.

After a day's walking I entered a cafe and, sitting at an empty table, spotted a full English breakfast only half eaten. Thinking of my hungry dog tied up outside, I scraped the food into an empty picnic box.

Imagine my horror when a man emerged from the Gents and came to my table to finish his meal.

Margaret Allen
Strines, Cheshire

A WALK A DAY...

SIR – You report that researchers at the University of
Cambridge have discovered that taking a brisk 20-minute walk
every day will help a person avoid the risk of early death. I first
heard this theory 40 years ago, when I was living in Chicago,
and I began an appropriate programme with my golden
retriever at my side. Ten minutes into the third day, the dog
died.

I have not walked briskly since, and if I abstain for two more
months, I hope to reach my 84th birthday.

> **Derek Gregory**
> Castle Cary, Somerset

SIR – I have noticed a worrying new trend of dog owners who
refuse to leave their cars when walking their dogs. They drive
slowly behind their canine while said dog takes itself for a walk.

> **George Owen**
> Salisbury, Wiltshire

SIR – Your correspondent recently encountered a dog bearing
a light. Near where I live, on the recreation ground after
dark, it's common to see lights moving at varying speeds and
directions, accompanied by a greenish glow moving along a
more constant pathway.

These are illuminated dogs and their mobile phone-bearing owners, doing evening walkies.

Dennis Gibson
Letchworth Garden City, Hertfordshire

SIR – During a rewarding holiday spent with grandchildren, Elizabeth, the six-year-old, on a walk with the dog, informed us that 'the ground is like a dog's computer and when Jess stops to sniff, she is collecting her emails.'

When Elizabeth is a grandparent, one wonders what technology she will be informed about.

Janet Jackson
Lincoln

SIR – Your correspondent is a bit harsh in suggesting that a roller-skating dog-walker should be banned from owning a dog.

Watch a sled team, tugging eagerly to set off for mile after mile. Or watch hill farmers on quad-bikes, accompanied by their dogs running with them over great distances.

Dogs are pack animals that love running with their 'pack'. Both my last Border collies loved running as I cycled over the Yorkshire Dales.

Sqn Ldr Jerry Riley
South Queensferry, Lothian

SIR – My wife's favoured friend Buster, a cross-breed sheepdog Labrador, developed a liking for collecting pheasants during his daily walk across Calke Park in Derbyshire, never challenged by the gamekeeper.

A business move took us back to the Midlands, near to a golf course, and a small reward on bringing his first golf ball altered Buster's choice of target.

During the last five years of his life, we counted more than 15,000 golf balls salvaged from Buster. Only one was taken in play – the golfer, whom we compensated with 12 balls, replied: 'I'd rather have the dog.' The vet was also paid in balls.

Paul Hickman
Melbourne, Derbyshire

SIR – Nigel Farndale writes that it is impossible to imagine taking a cat for a walk.

We have had two cats that enjoyed walks. Tommers came only if the dog came. Tiggerpuss came regardless, and would walk any distance across fields, but if we went to the village, she stopped and waited on a wall for us to get back from the shop (or pub).

Nigel and his cat should get out more.

Chris James
Abergele, Clwyd

FOR THE LOVE OF DOG

SIR – Whenever I read about Damien Hirst, I cannot help but remember one day in September last year. I was picking blackberries behind his studio in Gloucestershire when Mungo, my black Labrador, went missing. I had to call him for about 20 minutes before he finally reappeared, but, whenever I drive past that spot, I have this terrible vision of my dog suspended in formaldehyde.

Tiffany Beilby
London W6

POOPER SWOOPERS

SIR – One day I took my St Bernard for a walk along the Dover sea front and he unfortunately added to the considerable mess that was already there. To my embarrassment I found I had forgotten to bring the appropriate plastic bag, so I hurried back to my car and drove him home.

I felt so guilty about this that I armed myself with the necessary accoutrements and returned to the sea front until I found the prize specimen worthy of a St. Bernard.

I told my wife who thought it so funny that she told all her friends. I couldn't see the joke until my wife explained that she didn't want to be associated with a crackpot who might be seen walking around without a dog looking for the best specimens to take home.

Dr R.J. Thompson
Guston, Kent

SIR — I, too, am annoyed by the sight of abandoned poo bags, but what can happen is that dog walkers put them down intending to collect them on the way back, then forget.

I know because I have done this myself, so now I keep the bag with me, sometimes absent-mindedly twirling it at speed round my fingers, causing concern to passers-by.

Sally Mander
Evesham, Worcestershire

SIR — Last week I found a bag of dog mess in my back garden at a distance of 100ft from the roadside. The same type of bag and mess appeared yesterday on my front drive.

I am concerned that the responsible person's throwing arm may have suffered an injury.

Martin Bastone
East Grinstead, West Sussex

ASLEEP WITHOUT LEAVE

SIR – Not only were donkeys used in Cyprus on anti-terrorist operations in the 1950s, as you report, we also had a particularly useless St Bernard.

After initial enthusiasm, he would lose interest and, on one memorable occasion, returned to camp at Stroumbi draped, blissfully sleeping, on the shoulders of four gunners.

B.D. Clark
Newcastle, Staffordshire

CREAM TEA FOR TWO

SIR – I was amused to read W.F. Deedes's column about Lady Munnings's dog, Black Knight.

As Royal Academy students, we were allowed to attend the grand summer soirees in the upstairs gallery, and would see Violet Munnings eating strawberries and ice cream, feeding Black Knight with the same spoon.

How sad that the RA is bereft of such characters nowadays.

Edna Weiss
London NW11

SIR — Lady Munnings's devotion to Black Knight continued in the dog's afterlife. On an occasion when she and I took afternoon tea together at Brown's Hotel, a silent, glassy-eyed Black Knight peered at us from his carrying-bag. It was only when he ignored the biscuits she offered him that I realised he had paid a visit to the taxidermist.

So far as I am aware, his memoirs, with which she assisted him, were never published, a loss both to the canine and human worlds.

John Nunneley
Petersham, Surrey

CUPBOARD LOVE

SIR — As an owner of a Border collie, I can confirm your report that 'the breed has a natural inclination to bond closely with one person' — to the person currently filling the dog's dinner bowl.

Andrew M. Birt
Guildford, Surrey

SIR – I am amazed that staff of Battersea Dogs' Home should have been surprised at the escapalogical feats of Red the lurcher, believing that 'these dogs are not renowned for their intelligence'.

The whole point of lurchers is to cross a bright working dog, such as a Border collie, with a less clever sight-hound, for example a greyhound, thus trading a few mph for improved intelligence and scenting ability in the progeny.

One of my lurchers once dislodged the hemispherical cover from a porting half-stilton, nibbled a layer of crust from the entire circumference, then nudged the cover back on to hide the deed.

We discovered it only when putting the cheese on the table at the end of a dinner party, when the dog simultaneously flung himself at my feet for mercy. Fortunately, both cheese and guests had soaked up enough port by then for our enjoyment to be unaffected.

Ian Hamilton Fazey
Liverpool

SIR — You report a star-nosed mole that can identify food and eat it in one-thousandth of a second. What kept it? We have a Labrador, Ben, who, in a similar time, can identify anything edible, awaken from a deep sleep, shoot across the kitchen, devour the food and return to his basket, all without appearing to be in a particular hurry.

He would probably eat a star-nosed mole, provided it looked like a biscuit.

Chris Middleton
Rotherham, South Yorkshire

SIR — I doubt that badgers are responsible for the decrease in the toad population. The common toad has glands that secrete a poisonous chemical that a badger would find disgusting.

My Labrador once licked a toad, then spent the next half hour frothing at the mouth. The toad walked away unhurt.

William Rusbridge
Tregony, Cornwall

A BITTER PILL

SIR – I was disgusted to read reports of a dog at Crufts being given poison-laced meat. I dearly hope the culprit is found, if only to learn his technique, since I can't even get my dog to take his worming tablets, however I conceal them.

Ian Eyres
Llanyblodwel, Shropshire

SIR – I concur with your correspondent about administering pills to dogs in a piece of cheese. However, I disagree with the variety. Cheddar can be rather crumbly, and an intelligent dog will separate the cheese from the medicine, subsequently depositing the unpalatable tablet elsewhere.

An over-ripe bit of brie rind is sufficiently smelly to confuse their excellent olfactory system, and adheres to the pill like glue.

Christine Hartridge
Hambledon, Hampshire

SIR – Our dog loves to steal the cat's food – that is where we hide his pill. Works every time.

Janet Croome
Truro, Cornwall

THE GREAT CAT VS DOG DEBATE

SIR — Britain has become a nation of cat owners. Is that because cats know their rights whereas dogs do their duty?

James Goodwin
Exeter

SIR — We all know that dogs have owners and cats have staff.

Professor John L. Burton
North Perrott, Somerset

SIR — It is not just the dominance of children that creates slaves to love. We have become butler and ladies' maid to our large St Bernard. Among our many chores is to be called from our bed at 3am to lift food from his bowl so that he may be hand-fed, then turn the bathroom tap so he may wash it down with running water.

Despite a really determined fight, we have succumbed to his emperor complex.

Christopher Conbeer
Colyton, Devon

SIR – I have tried for years to train our spaniel to come when I whistle, but to no avail. Our tabby cat comes running straight away.

David Aston
Shackleford, Surrey

SIR – Surely dogs are better than cats or humans.

Come home an hour late from the pub with a cold dinner on the table. Wife, cat, dog – which is pleased to see you?

Nairn Lawson
Portbury, Somerset

SIR – Cats' intelligence far exceeds that of dogs. Take our Bengal cat Zoe. She operates the DVD player, the waste disposal button and the patio door, and she is a reliable alarm clock; she can hold an erudite conversation on most subjects and laughs at Ed Miliband.

Not even an educated Border collie could match that.

Jeremy Jacobs
Woking, Surrey

SIR – Dogs are chipped for identification and their poo has to be collected wherever it may fall.

Cat owners have no such concerns. Their pets roam free, kill what they want and poo where they please – preferably in a neighbour's garden, so they do not give away their home's location to theoretical predators.

How blessed are they that purr.

Julian Barnes
Bodfari, Denbighshire

SIR – Samuel Pepys's friend Dr Williams defended his garden with a dog that 'do kill all the cats that come hither to kill his pigeons, and do afterwards bury them; and do it with so much care that they shall be quite covered; that if but the tip of the tail hangs out he will take up the cat again, and dig the hole deeper'.

Dr N.G. McCrum
Oxford

SIR — Regarding your report about what makes a gentleman, it was disappointing to discover that both Sir Winston Churchill and Dr Johnson fell at the final hurdle, having both owned a cat.

Philip Tucker
Brighton, East Sussex

SIR — For a well-adjusted personality, a human needs to reside with both a dog and a cat. A dog makes you feel like God and a cat ensures you know you are not.

Judy Knipe
Kelvedon, Essex

SIR — Our two rescue dogs, Flossie and Sally, have been following with great interest the recent correspondence in praise of cats to the detriment of dogs. What they would like to know is, if cats are so marvellous, where are the guide cats to the blind, sniffer cats, mountain rescue cats, police cats, and home-aid cats to the elderly?

In their opinion, cats kill songbirds and are only fit to chase.

John Chapman
Sowerby Bridge, West Yorkshire

BY LOYAL APPOINTMENT

SIR — Would a guide dog be of use to Prince Philip, given his propensity to unfortunate remarks? Perhaps a trained corgi, ready to nip.

Rosemary Papaeliou
Broadstone, Dorset

SIR — The Queen's love of horses and dogs is well known, but what about cats? Have the corgis made Buckingham Palace a cat-free zone?

Gillian Dunstan
Witnesham, Suffolk

SIR — It is obvious why there are no cats at Buckingham Palace. Every cat I have known considers itself to be royalty and would insist on appearing on the balcony on all royal occasions. At which time it would turn its back on the cheering crowds and ignore them.

George Sizeland
Carterton, Oxfordshire

SIR — My parents attended the wedding of Princess Elizabeth and Prince Philip (with whom my father had served in the Royal Navy during the war). Later that day we were among the crowds in front of the Palace waiting to see the newlyweds on the balcony. Suddenly a cat appeared and walked along the balustrade to a massive cheer from the waiting crowds.

Violet Hooper
Yatton, Somerset

SIR — In his autobiography, Christopher Robin Milne described his mother and father as, respectively, a cat person and a dog person.

'My mother was like a cat. She responded to the beauty, the peace and the solitude that is offered [in the country]. Once, when she was going for a walk, I asked if I could come with her. "No", she said "but come and meet me on my way back."

'My father was surely a dog... it had to be a proper walk, a walk with a purpose, planned beforehand, worked out on a map even. And you couldn't go alone; you had to be with somebody... Like a dog, too, he was happiest when chasing a ball.'

Elisabeth Everitt
Swaffham Prior, Cambridgeshire

SIR — Given the lack of suitable candidates for the Nobel Peace Prize in 2012 I would like to nominate my dog, Lassie, and next door's cat, Sammy Fudge. They spent a lifetime chasing, scratching and warring, but in recent years have relinquished hostilities and co-exist on the carpet together.

Keith R. Ashworth-Lord
Rochdale, Lancashire

CATS AND THEIR CURIOSITIES

'I'm not handing any more powers to you. IN or OUT?'

CURIOSITY FED THE CAT

SIR – 'Turn the oven off, leaving the door ajar, and leave the chicken to rest for at least 15 minutes before carving'. Simon Hopkinson, who chefs and fellow food writers decided has written the most useful cookery book of all time, may know how to cook perfect roast chicken but he has clearly never owned a cat.

Dr Hilary Aitken
Kilmacolm, Inverness

SIR – A cat stuck up a tree, costing £400 an hour to rescue, reminded me of advice I was given by a group who helped the fire brigade rescue cats.

They told me to put pilchards at the foot of the tree that our cat had been meowing from for hours. He was down in minutes.

Anne Grice
London SW14

SIR – When purchasing cat food you have a wide choice of flavours: beef, chicken, salmon, lamb and so on. Why is there no bird or mouse flavour?

Mike Stoner
Wokingham, Berkshire

LETTING SLIP THE CATS OF WAR

SIR — I have two cats in my house and no mice. I could make a significant saving in food and veterinary bills if I reduced the cat order of battle by 50 per cent, but I suspect that the mice would gain the upper hand, as one cat cannot patrol the house and garden all the time.

The Chancellor and defence planners are 'situating the appreciation' [in their attempt to introduce defence cuts] as it is known in the Armed Forces — bending the facts to suit what one wishes will happen, rather than anticipating what may happen.

Lt Cdr Ben Bosley RN (retd)
London SE7

SIR — Lt Cdr Bosley's battalion of cats must be of a different breed from mine.

I had no mouse trouble — until I got cats. They catch them, bring them in, then release them to play chase in the house.

I have even seen one cat watch a brave mouse scurry across the floor, and lift his lazy, feline head as if to say: 'Inside — not my job.'

Or perhaps Lt Cdr Bosley has drilled his cats in naval discipline?

Dr Jim Finlayson
Beauly, Inverness

SIR — When an adjoining field became a mass of molehills, invasion seemed inevitable. But, as I dejectedly contemplated the first eruption my side of the hedge, my Siamese cat pawed aside the soft earth, and peed in the hole. No more moles.

Bridget King
Cookham, Berkshire

SIR — May I congratulate your columnist Sam Leith on sharing his home with such an excellent mouser.

I, too, have a cat that has dealt with the mouse element in my flat, although thankfully, in her case, rather than placing it under my pillow, she left the corpse on the bathroom floor.

Mr Leith should not be dismayed by the actions of his feline friend. She was, in fact, looking after him, for, contrary to widespread belief, she was not bringing the mouse to him as a gift. Rather, she was teaching him how to hunt, a talent — who knows? — he may have to employ one day.

Virginia Blackburn
London W14

SIR — Regarding mice as presents: get husband to separate resentful cat from mouse. Lock cat and husband in nearby room. Choose husband's softest, comfiest and roomiest slipper. Present slipper enticingly to mouse. Mouse will run into slipper. Leave slipper and occupant in mouse-friendly part of garden for at least an hour. Leave cat (and possibly husband) in nearby room for at least an hour. Pacify cat with salmon. Pacify husband with whatever works for him. Possibly salmon.

Carol Pearce
Colwall, Worcestershire

SIR — A friend has found that if she sprays her cat's victims with hair spray, the panicking mice slow down enough to enable her to catch them and return them to the wild.

M. Pascoe
Apremont, France

CAT VS RAT

SIR – I'm afraid that Number 10 may be barking up the wrong tree in adopting a cat to deal with rats. Cats catch mice, but mostly avoid rats.

I have known only one cat in my life who would catch rats, and we always suspected that he was at least part panther.

What Downing Street needs is a small terrier, preferably of no distinguishable breed. It will be boisterous, and probably rather noisy, but should eventually do the trick.

Sally Gibbons
London SW19

SIR – When I was a child, my mother always wore her wedding dress for a dinner party on her wedding anniversary.

One year while she was cooking, my brother ran in to say there was a rat in the chicken run. She stuffed her dress into her stocking tops, grabbed a pitchfork from the stable and rushed to kill the rat before returning to finish cooking dinner.

She claimed she was probably the only person to have killed a rat while wearing a wedding dress.

Mary Still
Bordon, Hampshire

SIR — Rather than a cat, David Cameron should acquire a dachshund.

When we moved house, we were alarmed to find that there was a rats' nest under an old coal bunker in the garden. My mother came to stay, bringing her dachshund. The dog quickly got down to business, patiently sitting by the bunker for most of the day. The score by evening was 12 rats.

When living in Singapore, enjoying a sundowner on a friend's veranda, I watched their dachshund kill a cobra that had been hiding behind a plant pot. It was all over in seconds.

Faith Harris
Slindon, West Sussex

SIR — I suggest that Cabinet ministers consider another means of expulsion known to their counterparts in early Scottish parliaments.

They should establish a herd of goats in the garden of Number 10. Rats detest goats; they do not infest or even appear in a house where one is living — doubtless the strong smell of the goats is too much for them.

Iain Thornber
Oban, Argyll

SIR — Am I the only one to be delighted that, after the 2015 general election, the occupant of Number 10 remains the same? I refer, of course, to Larry the cat.

He looked very pleased with himself on the doorstep last Friday evening, and completely upstaged Fiona Bruce doing her bit to the camera.

Michael Forward
Great Bookham, Surrey

RIP, PRIME MOUSER

SIR — I was saddened to learn of the death of Humphrey, the Number 10 cat, who was so shamefully ejected by the Blair family after they moved in.

I cannot help but think that, with his acute feline sense of smell, he would have been alert to something fishy going on (nay, even smelling the odd rat) and thus been of enormous use in keeping Downing Street wholesome, as this appears to have eluded the senior echelons of the Labour Party.

Roger Botha
Bromsgrove, Worcestershire

SIR – Humphrey, the Chief Mouser, reminded me of an incident some years ago when I was working in a settlement house in Bethnal Green, London. The house cat needed veterinary treatment. The fees were paid out of the house expenses. Problem: how to enter that to satisfy the auditors? Solution: essential repairs to mouse trap. The auditors were quite satisfied.

Mary Code
St Albans, Hertfordshire

SIR – In the days before it was possible for anyone to wander up Downing Street, two female American tourists did just that. Humphrey was let out of the front door, sniffed at their lower limbs, then strolled on.

The tourists approached the police officer guarding Number 10 and said they were amazed at the low level of security in comparison with the USA. The officer informed them that they had, in fact, been checked by a covert system. They looked around, bemused.

'That cat you just saw is a specially trained Metropolitan Police cat,' he explained. 'It can detect, by smell, firearms and explosives and, should you have had either, would have warned me.'

So, perhaps Humphrey did go into an honourable semi-retirement, training other cats in weapons detection skills. But we would never know, would we?

Chris Walker
London SW19

SIR — Chris Walker has, I fear, got the wrong cat. It could not have been Humphrey in the era of unrestricted public access to Downing Street. It must have been Wilberforce.

I am not aware that Wilberforce was trained by the Metropolitan Police in firearms and explosives detection. I do know that Margaret Thatcher was relaxed about the security of this secret weapon, if that is what he was, because she bought him a tin of sardines in a Moscow supermarket, since that was about all there was to buy in it.

I can also testify that Wilberforce was a normal cat. He gave me, an asthmatic, much trouble on Monday mornings after spending the weekend, between anti-mouse operations, lounging on my desk.

Sir Bernard Ingham
Purley, Surrey

ABLE SEACAT

SIR – Among the injured crew of HMS *Amethyst*, whose attack in 1949 by Chinese forces is commemorated this week, was Able Seaman Simon.

Twenty-five members were killed and many wounded. Simon, the ship's cat, was hit in the leg by shrapnel and his whiskers and fur burnt off. The crew found him a place in the sick bay, where he took to visiting the injured sailors, comforting them by kneading their chests and purring.

The *Amethyst*'s captain, John Kerans, nominated him for the PDSA Dickin Medal for bravery. It had regularly been awarded to dogs and pigeons, but never a cat.

Val Lewis
London EC2

FELINE HYPERTENSION

SIR – 'Owning a cat cuts stroke risks'? On the contrary, I know many people who own cats and they often have a stroke.

Rev Brendan Killeen
East Hunsbury, Northamptonshire

SIR — Owning a cat may reduce the risk of a stroke, but, as the neighbour of cat-owners, my risk of a stroke increases dramatically every time their cats use my garden as a lavatory.

Brian Hallam
Burton-upon-Trent, Staffordshire

SIR — There is a cheap and effective answer to this problem. Put some used teabags in a screw-top jar and spray liberally with an aerosol can of Deep Heat. Shake well, then place the tea bags where the cats normally enter. They do not like it.

David Craddock
Radstock, Somerset

SIR — During the Second World War scientists developing radar found that their cooling mugs of tea reheated when left on a particular piece of equipment. This phenomenon resulted in the ubiquitous microwave — good, clear, logical development of a casual observation.

So how on earth did David Craddock discover that spraying used tea bags with Deep Heat was a good cat deterrent?

Robert Warner
West Woodhay, Berkshire

SIR – You warn of future robotic machines capable of smashing the Earth to pieces.

I'll start to worry about this threat once there's an artificial intelligence gadget clever enough to find and clean our cat's litter tray.

Neil Richardson
Kirkheaton, West Yorkshire

PUTTING THE CAT OUT

SIR – I watched the video of the woman putting the cat into the wheelie-bin and was horrified.

The green bin? Surely it should have gone in the brown one.

Ewan Dance
London SE18

WHODUNNIT SOLVED

SIR — The report regarding the hazardous relationship between cats and lilies has solved a 50-year-old mystery. Our next-door neighbour's cat, a daily visitor, was found unconscious in our flower beds and, despite desperate attempts to revive him, faded away before our eyes.

Several months went by, and then the neighbour's new cat almost suffered the same fate. Fortunately, he survived.

It seemed clear that a poisoner was at work and our suspicion fell on an elderly man who was known to dislike cats.

Then came the 1953 flood. Our gardens were submerged under several inches of sea water and one flower that failed to re-appear in the summer was the tiger lily.

They were not replaced and there were no more premature cat deaths — but, sadly, old Mr Croad was still 'in Coventry' when he died a few months later.

Bernard Rickwood
Sheerness, Kent

RAC, MOTHER

SIR — We arranged for the order of service at my mother's funeral to end with the not unusual phrase, 'Requiescat in pace'.

Mourners at Brompton Oratory were probably surprised to find that, far from wanting to rest in peace, my mother's dying wish was, 'Requires a cat'.

Christopher Batchelor
Penrith, Cumbria

HOME IS WHERE THE CAT IS

SIR — I would be sceptical of any study suggesting that cats do not miss their owners, as you report.

When we return from a couple of days away, having left our cat in a warm, comfortable conservatory with an automatic feeder and access to the garden, she runs to meet the car and then flops over into a ridiculous supine position, waiting to be fussed over.

She then becomes excited and runs all over the house at top speed — quite the opposite of her usual dignified, slightly superior demeanour.

Gillian Hyde
Potters Bar, Middlesex

SIR — Our current family pets — a pair of boisterous tabbies — attempt to secrete themselves inside our luggage whenever they detect us packing to go away.

Louise Buxton
Bath

CASBOS

SIR — If a dog that chases a cat can get a 'dogbo', what about a cat that kills a bird?

Georgie Helyer
Hanging Langford, Wiltshire

SIR — While living in Cape Town, my daughter's cat was the subject of an ASBO at the request of the neighbours, whose own cat was supposedly being terrorised by our moggy.

Ours was only allowed out in the daytime between 2pm and 5pm.

Try explaining that to a cat.

Tina Peacock-Edwards
Crowthorne, Berkshire

SIR — You quote a report on the website of the Royal Society for the Protection of Birds as saying: 'It is likely that most of the birds killed by cats would have died anyway from other causes.'

Does this mean that some of the birds not killed by cats are immortal?

Brian Smith
Dunfermline, Fife

SIR — My Siamese cat, who is a dedicated hunter, met her match when she took a youngster from a blackbird's nest in the neighbouring garden.

Blackbirds came out in force to chase her. They now operate a lookout near the cat flap and, when my cat appears, one bird alarms the others and the noise continues until she retreats.

Margaret Draper
Salisbury, Wiltshire

SIR — The birds on the birdsong disc last weekend in the *Telegraph* are arranged alphabetically. Upon hearing the seventh track, the blackbird, my two cats raced in and tried to get to the speaker on the wall.

If I play the whole disc, will the cats identify all the birds that visit my garden? Also, would a CD of common garden birds, played frequently, eventually desensitise the cats, since they would hear the song, but not enjoy the reward of the chase?

Fiona McKenzie
Blisworth, Northamptonshire

'Another bird is
tormenting our cat'

FEATHERED
FRIENDS

'We're fracking for worms'

ELECTING A NATIONAL BIRD FOR BRITAIN

SIR — Perhaps the general election could decide the national bird for Britain.

If the Conservatives win — blue tit; Labour — red-legged partridge; Lib Dem — yellowhammer; UKIP — purple heron; Greens — green finch; SNP — northern gannet.

David Barlow
Cury, Cornwall

SIR — Most people only know the red grouse from its depiction on whisky bottles, so it is probably not the best candidate for Britain's national bird.

The strongest contender must be the mute swan — graceful and serene, but very aggressive when threatened.

Major General Bryan Webster (retd)
Ewshot, Hampshire

SIR – When I was at primary school we were taught that the wren is the national bird because it inhabits all parts of Britain, it keeps itself to itself, and is self-effacing.

Hence it was chosen to appear on the farthing coin to illustrate British virtues.

Ron Mason
East Grinstead, West Sussex

SIR – Perhaps a budgie would be appropriate. These days most of the nation seems to spend its time tweeting, 'Who's a pretty boy, then?'

Elizabeth Davy
Kirkby Stephen, Cumbria

SIR – My immediate thought was the great bustard. The initials – GB – would be easy for the public to recall.

Mike Elliott
Dore, Sheffield

SIR – Last week I saw in my garden robins, great tits, blue tits, chaffinches, dunnocks, thrushes, blackbirds, ringnecked doves, wood pigeons, jackdaws, a wren and a pheasant.

However, the only one who sings throughout the winter is the robin. That gets my vote.

Candy Haley
Cobham, Surrey

SIR – We already have a lion with, if necessary, a unicorn for backup. That must surely trump the robin.

Steve McWeeney
Morpeth, Northumberland

SIR – A poll has confirmed the robin as Britain's 'national bird'.

I fear international derision at the idea that a country with pretensions to a leading world position has chosen a 'little dicky bird' instead of, say, a barn owl (wisdom) or a golden eagle (power and might).

George Stebbing-Allen
Wigginton, Hertfordshire

SIR — George Stebbing-Allen criticises the choice of a 'little dicky-bird' as a national bird for Britain.

Norway is home to 10,000 whitetailed eagles, birds with a wingspan of seven feet. Yet the national bird of Norway is the whitethroated dipper, a bird just seven inches long.

Anne Jago
Levens, Cumbria

BIRDIE!

SIR — The picture of a crow flying off with a golf ball in its beak reminded me of an experience many years ago at the Walmer and Kingsdown Golf Club in Kent.

I was playing in a Sunday morning fourball and was driving off from the 18th tee. The 18th at Kingsdown was a longish par five, and as my ball bounced and rolled down the fairway, a seagull swooped down, picked it up in its beak, flew on and — lo and behold! — dropped it on the green.

We were all in fits of laughter at this, but had no idea what the ruling was. So we consulted the Pro, a lovely man called J.W. Robinson. His ruling was that, as the ball was in motion when the seagull picked it up, any additional yardage provided by the unwitting bird could reasonably be counted as part of my drive. (The outside agency rule only applied if the ball was stationary.)

This is the only time I have ever driven the green on a par five. I missed the putt for an albatross but I did get a birdie.

James Little
Alresford, Hampshire

SIR – Your correspondent implies that golf courses are environmentally barren and free of wildlife. She suggests that if green belt sites must be built on, then golf courses should be considered.

The course that I play on has large areas of 'rough' where larks nest in the spring. There are many other breeds of birds, including sparrows, martins, woodpeckers, pheasant and birds of prey such as kestrel and red kite; so there must be an ample supply of food for them, such as voles, shrews and mice.

I also regularly see hares and rabbits and have had a muntjac deer run past me. There is a wide range of flora, and the ponds contain large carp.

Do we really want to see this wildlife haven concreted over and built on?

John Stephens
Bicester, Oxfordshire

SIR – At Swinton Park Golf Club for the past few years, crows have been stealing balls. Indeed, sometimes three out of four are stolen.

According to experts, the crow is the easiest bird to train, which suggests that some nefarious person may be making a living out of club members.

Ernie Rimmer
Salford, Lancashire

A WING AND A FLARE

SIR – When I was camping once near Corfe Castle, a crow entered the open tent and seized the match that I had used to light the Primus stove and shoved it, still lit, under its wing. I lit another and it repeated the process under the other wing.

Was it a variant of 'anting', in which the crow uses the formic acid from ants to kill pests under its feathers?

Robert Sunderland
Little Wymondley, Hertfordshire

SIR — Birds picking up discarded cigarette ends and using them to fumigate their wings for parasites is not that unusual.

In 1956, in a chapter 'The Remarkable History of Bird Anting', in his book *Animal Legends*, the British zoologist Maurice Burton noted: 'We have recorded instances of birds that will pick up a lighted cigarette from an ashtray and hold the smouldering end to the undersides of the wings.'

Rod Preece
Ontario, Canada

WINGED MIRRORS

SIR — Recently, we have had a male chaffinch pecking glass which was leaning against a shed. When the glass was removed he took to sitting on the car door and attacking the wing mirror.

He persisted despite attempts to drive him away, so we have now fitted a mirror on the fence post to divert his attention.

Valerie Osenton
Cooling, Kent

FEATHERED FRIENDS

SIR — We have seen a rook busily tearing the lead strips away from windows. They move from one to another. We hope that lead poisoning will eventually solve the problem.

Mike Lander
Fishbourne, West Sussex

SIR — We have a lesser-spotted woodpecker who regularly attacks our weather-vane pole. The noise it makes is like a machine gun being fired. He must have a terrible headache as the pole is made of metal.

Jonathan Godrich
Craven Arms, Shropshire

SIR — Here in Suffolk I have a bigger problem. Every morning, without fail, a cock pheasant hurls himself at my glass external doors. This extraordinary behaviour lasts for an hour from sunrise.

My late mother believed that we 'came back' as birds, so I am somewhat loath to do anything drastic. I grit my teeth, smile and wave.

Heather M. Tanner
Earl Soham, Suffolk

SIR – There used to be a Dorset belief that a bird tapping at the window augured a death.

On April 20, 1935, Lawrence of Arabia complained of 'a beastly tit' banging itself against a downstairs window of his cottage at Clouds Hill, Dorset.

'First I thought he was a bird-pressman, trying to get a story: then a narcissist, admiring his figure in the glass. Now I think he is just mad.'

Lawrence was apparently 'almost driven wild' by the bird, which a neighbour described as 'hammering eerily on the windows'.

On May 13, Lawrence suffered his fatal motorcycle accident near the cottage, dying on May 19. The bird, which by then had been hammering at the glass for at least four weeks, for six hours a day, was shot.

Graham Chainey
Brighton, East Sussex

SIR – A fortnight ago a pheasant crashed through our window, sending shards flying across the room. The bird fell dead on the carpet shortly after.

Last week the alarm went off in the early morning. It was a jackdaw that had entered through the (capped) chimney. Later that day the alarm went off again. I rushed home and made a thorough inspection. Upstairs I found two jackdaws on my dressing table.

Are we unlucky to have had three avian intrusions so close together?

Rosemary Morton Jack
Oddington, Oxfordshire

SIR – Rosemary Morton Jack reports three break-ins by birds.

A few weeks ago I was sitting in my study when a white bundle fell past the window. There was a thump and the sound of breaking glass. I rushed into my sitting room to find the stained-glass window shattered and the lead work twisted. A swan stared back at me with a cross expression.

What is more, I can report that 25 years ago another swan fell at the exact same spot and broke the same stained-glass window. What freak of chance is that?

Colin Gillespie
Wells, Somerset

SIR — I have made cut-outs of a swallow in flight in black shiny paper and pasted them onto the windows. There have been no casualties this year.

L. Campkin
Hexham, Northumberland

SIR — Your correspondence about birds flying into windows reminds me of when we lived in a Queen Anne manor house, the original windows of which were largely intact, and much treasured.

Having been out for the day, my wife and I came home to find a window smashed and a dead pheasant lying in the middle of the dining-room floor.

It was only years later, at my son's wedding, that his best man and co-conspirator told of the day when, playing cricket on the lawn, one of them had put a ball through the window. In order to avoid repercussions, my son had run out and shot a pheasant to replace the cricket ball among the pile of broken glass.

Hardly surprising that he went on to enjoy a successful military career.

Dennis Wombell
Menthorpe, North Yorkshire

PESTILENT PARAKEETS

SIR — I sat down to write this letter at six-thirty in the morning, bedroom windows open to enjoy a lovely summer's day and the sound of birdsong.

But all I could hear was the screeching of parakeets, which have driven away the indigenous songbirds. Will nobody rid me of these pestilent birds?

Tony Parrack
London SW20

SIR — On looking through my grandmother's cookbook by Mrs Beeton, there is a recipe for parakeet pie.

Brian R. Fokes
Rottingdean, East Sussex

SIR —There are colonies of parakeets nesting in the trees near the seaward end of La Rambla in Barcelona.

While we were enjoying a recent lunch at a restaurant, one of their more inquisitive and noisy number almost drowned in the ornamental pool next to our table. It was rescued by a Spanish couple, who wrapped it in a sweater and fed it.

Lunchtime entertainment was seldom bettered.

John Garrett
Newcastle upon Tyne

SIR – Leave the parakeets alone. Although they screech, they are pretty and, as far as I can see, harmless.

They do not take eggs and young birds, as does the exploding population of magpies, crows and grey squirrels. They eat mainly seeds and fruit.

Cull the magpies and crows instead and I am sure the population of garden birds would increase.

Jill Thorne
Felpham, West Sussex

SIR — Does ITV have a keeper who might dispose of the chattering magpie that is so evident in most outdoor scenes of *Downton Abbey*?

Lance Warrington
Northleach, Gloucestershire

SIR — A magpie once spied our lurcher on our back lawn chewing away at a raw bone. The bird landed about 5ft in front of her and decided upon a strategy for getting at the bone. The magpie hopped, in a semi-circle, around the dog and, when safely behind her, very sharply pecked the dog's tail. It had the desired result as the dog jumped up with a yelp and ran indoors, leaving the magpie to feed on the bone for a few seconds.

Robert Vickers
Holmfirth, West Yorkshire

COMPETITIVE BIRD FEEDING

SIR – Bird feeding where we live is competitive. Our birds demand not only what they like, but the best possible quality. Otherwise, they're off down the street.

Sunflower seeds have to be dehusked, for instance. Our goldfinches will take niger, but only occasionally. Peanuts are the favourite of almost all of our tits, but not from wire nut-feeders. Long-tailed tits prefer fat slabs. Blackcaps and starlings favour those with added insects.

A real winter treat for goldfinches are the seeds from *verbena bonariensis*.

Arthur Sotheran
Bristol

SIR – Why are garden birds so frightened of human beings?

I provide food and water for them, show them nothing but kindness, and yet they fly off as soon as they see me coming.

Robins seem to be the most fearless – why? Blackbirds show a certain insouciance; pigeons, sparrows and tits are hopelessly jittery. I may not be St Francis, but why can't they trust me a bit more?

Jeremy Nicholas
Great Bardfield, Essex

SIR – If I were approached by a being 25 times taller than me, even if it offered me a plate of my favourite food, I, too, would grab it and run.

P.J. Reardon
Tonbridge, Kent

SIR – Our tame blackbird is completely fearless and has precise dietary requirements: three grapes cut in half, no more no less, and possibly some sultanas. When her children were born, some cat food did not go amiss.

She also enjoys the worms and slugs, properly crushed, that my wife provides.

Martin Greenwood
Fringford, Oxfordshire

SIR – My 1909 copy of *British Birds in their Haunts* by Rev. C.A. Johns describes the blackbird as 'suspicious and wary; however hard pressed he may be by hunger, you will rarely see him hunting for food in the open field. He prefers the solitude and privacy of the bush.'

How many generations of blackbirds have occurred to make this change?

Ursula Marriage
West Chiltington, West Sussex

SIR — One of our blackbirds was so keen for further supplies of sultanas that he ventured through the utility room, the kitchen and the dining room into our living room, where he cocked his head inquiringly until I got up to follow.

He gently hopped back out and waited for the food. He even left a charming thank-you note on the floor.

Rita and Donita Hosegood
Cookham, Berkshire

SIR — I have a robin that visits every morning, to be fed either cooked sausage meat or grated cheese. If I am not on time with the feeding, the robin will hop into the kitchen and perch on a dining chair.

Michele Cattell
Mollington, Cheshire

SIR — The reason why songbirds are so easily taken by magpies is because of the actions of so-called bird lovers, who feed them a totally inappropriate diet.

Like children fed entirely on burgers, these small birds become fat, sluggish and lazy: easy pickings for magpies and cats. If bird lovers wish to see more song birds, they should stop feeding them.

Andrew Seward
Taunton, Devon

EXHAUSTED SONGBIRDS

SIR – If the RSPB needs explanations for any demise of robins, blackbirds and song thrushes, I suggest it looks no further than the effect of utter exhaustion caused by competitive night-time singing competitions encouraged by urban light pollution.

Terry Morgan
Stroud, Gloucestershire

SIR – Is it any surprise that numbers of songbirds have fallen substantially in town gardens, when the trend for decking and paving is rife?

A bird-feeder is no substitute for trees, shrubs and grass. The tidy, zero-maintenance garden is, sadly, a sterile environment for birds.

Robert Gibbs
London N8

SIR – We normally have a wren, a robin and a couple of blackbirds in our small garden which leads down to the River Ribble, where there are always several ducks, a heron and a goose in residence. Therefore, it was with some expectation that we awaited bird census hour on Sunday.

The result — nothing. Is it possible that they were working together to establish themselves on the endangered species list?

David Maddison
Settle, North Yorkshire

SIR — I have also noticed a lack of birds in my garden during Birdwatch weekends. I suspect that they are not keen on having their details noted by the RSPB, just as I am not keen on having mine kept by the Government for identity card purposes.

Penelope Hurley
Dunmow, Essex

GREASEPROOF FOIL

SIR — To foil squirrels stealing from the birds we invested in a free-standing pole with peanut feeders hanging from the top of it. Within a day, we spotted one hanging from the metal feeding containers situated at the top of the stand.

Our answer was to grease the pole. The offending animal was seen sliding rapidly back down the pole, then walking across the lawn trying to wipe the grease from its feet.

Suzanne Lyons
Barnstaple, Devon

SIR — Peanut butter is good for squirrel traps, although it does not enjoy universal success.

When we tried it, each morning we would inspect our trap, which would invariably be occupied by the same large, contented hedgehog. Having finished the peanut butter, it would patiently await release, and its next free supper.

Like Fletcher in the *Porridge* series, it evidently regarded incarceration as an occupational hazard in a life of crime.

Dr Julian Critchlow
Tregaron, Ceredigion

THE JOCK AND THE BUBBLYJOCK

SIR — With reference to recent correspondence about 'bubblyjock', according to Lord Campbell's *Lives of the Lord Chancellors*, when Alexander Wedderburn, who became Lord High Chancellor of Great Britain in 1793, was three years old, he provoked a fierce turkey-cock by shouting at him: 'Bubbly Jock, bubbly Jock, your wife is a witch and she's going to be burnt with a barrel of pitch.'

The enraged bird flew at him and would have pecked his eyes out had his nurse not rescued him. Years later, when the gardener's boy who had witnessed the incident was taken to see the Lord Chancellor, he exclaimed: 'Weel! Weel! He may be a great man now, but I mind fine he was aince sair hadden doon by his mither's bubbly Jock!'

Margaret Evans
Worthing, West Sussex

PIGEON ENGLISH

SIR — Having lived in the South East and the South West, I do not believe there is a regional difference in the song of the wood pigeon, as some of your correspondents suggest. They all sing 'I love you, I do' as a stanza repeated a variable number of times.

The odd thing is that each bird ends with 'I' and, when starting again, continues with 'love you, I do'.

Pauline Craik
Portishead, Somerset

SIR – Every year on our farm we were visited by a pair of ring doves. Their conversation was always the same: 'I just don't want to. So please don't make me. I told you dar—ling. No!'

The reply in a lower key: 'Now come on sweet—ie. And don't be sil—ly. You know you want it. Now!'

Various pairs came and went but the conversation was always the same.

Elizabeth Higgs
Badlesmere, Kent

SIR – For the past few mornings, a pigeon in my garden has woken me at six o'clock by cooing: 'Come on, England'.

If he ever waves a red-and-white flag, he will be shot.

Peter Stockwell
Ely, Cambridgeshire

SIR – The wood pigeons in East Sussex coo: 'It's all right, Betty.' Even a local blackbird declares in his melodic repertoire: 'I want a bacon burger.'

Denis Jukes
Hastings, East Sussex

SIR — My grandfather told me that Taffy was waiting by the farm gate deciding which cow to steal, when a pigeon came along and said: 'Take two cows, Taffy.'

Richard Goodbourn
Keymer, West Sussex

SIR — A cock blackbird in my mother's garden learnt to imitate the two-note whistle that my late father and I used to do upon returning to the family house.

My elderly mother, while sitting in her garden and hearing my whistle, followed by the blackbird's, would chuckle, and say: 'Hello, dear. There's your father again.'

Graham Clifton
Kingston upon Thames, Surrey

SIR — As many of your readers will know, the starling is a great mimic. Years ago I stayed in a pub in Somerset and was awoken at 5am by the electronic sounds of the bar's fruit machine, only to discover that it was actually a beautiful starling singing away on the gutter outside my bedroom window. I was enthralled.

The blackbird is also capable of the same trick. For the last three years my wife and I have been entertained by a blackbird which includes in its glorious repertoire a perfect rendition of the whistle my wife uses to call her dog. This can lead to some confusion, however, as this is the same whistle my wife uses to summon me to the house.

Paul Sargeantson
Britwell Salome, Oxfordshire

SIR — We have a blackbird who includes my husband's mobile ringtone in his daily song.

I first heard it about four weeks ago, and thought it was my imagination, but now I hear him singing it every day.

Christina McAllister
Uttoxeter, Staffordshire

SIR — There is a blackbird living in our village that obviously keeps up to date with the latest technology.

It is able to mimic perfectly the sound of the Microsoft Windows start-up jingle.

Lesley Mackness
Tibberton, Shropshire

SIR — The wood pigeons in the Midlands are evidently more censorious than those in other parts. As I often find myself translating for my husband, their song is: 'The lawn needs cutting.'

Sylvia Holt
Sutton Cheney, Leicestershire

SIR — I can't help feeling that this correspondence suggests that birdsong is the acoustic version of the Rorschach test.

Ronald Walford
Darenth, Kent

NIGHTINGALE NEAR BERKELEY SQUARE

SIR — I'm sad for your correspondent losing her nightingales to development. She may be encouraged to hear that recently on two successive nights at Opera Holland Park at least two nightingales were singing in the gardens; one of them joined in with an aria in Don Pasquale.

I have seen a nightingale almost sitting in the auditorium and singing with the orchestra.

Joanna Strangwayes-Booth
Kettlestone, Norfolk

THE SECOND CUCKOO

SIR — Thomas Hardy observed that the surest sign of the arrival of spring was when indoor folk claimed to have heard the cuckoo and outdoor folk replied that they had heard him several days before.

Jim Doar
Winterborne Clenston, Dorset

SIR — Never mind the first cuckoo of spring, what about the first mosquito bite of summer? I have the itching to prove it, and the miscreant's corpse.

Jennifer Latham
Wedmore, Somers

SIR — When I was a child, the call of the cuckoo echoing through the woods was a sure sign that spring had arrived. Now I find that a more accurate measure of the seasons is the vote by members of the National Union of Teachers to go on strike.

Jonathan Fulford
Bosham, West Sussex

SIR — In my quarter of London, it is not the birds that are the harbingers of spring, but Australians. From my windows on Friday, I heard their first noisy party of the season. Spring is here.

Bryan Welch
London W6

HOW TO TRAIN A SEAGULL

SIR — Every year a pair of seagulls nests on my roof. Because my garden is the only feasible runway for the fledglings' maiden flight, they have, in the past, become nervous and aggressive. The reason they dive bomb is to make you go away.

However, it is easy to train them to desist. You simply stand with an umbrella while they attack, making eye contact after each sortie. After about half an hour (circa 60 flights) the exhausted bird will have received the message: you are not going to move.

They remember this from one year to the next and will not attack again.

Mark Hill
Seaford, East Sussex

FEATHERED FRIENDS

SIR — Every Monday at 6.30am my 85-year-old mother sits on a stool behind the hedge with a broom, waiting for seagulls to flip the lid of her wheelie bin and strew its contents across the road.

There should be a mandatory annual cull of these flying vermin before they take over Cornwall.

Jayne Roberts
Truro, Cornwall

SIR — Two gulls, a male and female, have visited our hilltop home in Brighton daily for nearly 20 years. Their appearance, gliding towards us and landing on our balcony railings, is a thing of beauty.

If we ignore them, the male will knock on the balcony door with his beak and wait for a hand-out. He once stepped inside, unnoticed, and waddled into the kitchen, unflappable but with no hint of aggression. We ushered him out of the back door and he flew away at peace with the world.

Allan Johns
Brighton, East Sussex

SIR — During the Second World War, marauding seagulls diving to snatch sandwiches were a nuisance to many coastal anti-aircraft and searchlight crews.

The problem was solved by letting them steal sandwiches laced with baking powder.

The seagulls, incapable of burping, soon got the message, and, being intelligent birds, quickly passed it on.

Kevin Heneghan
St Helens, Lancashire

SIR — The only time I can recall eating a pasty, I was sitting on a bench overlooking St Ives harbour.

Having consumed half of it, I was relieved when a seagull snatched the rest from my hand.

David Miller
Maidenhead, Berkshire

RESOURCEFUL HOME IMPROVEMENTS

SIR – Your correspondent's sighting of what might have been the last tape cassette in Britain reminded me of a resourceful blackbird which recycled a long length of cassette tape by using it to secure its nest in the climbing hydrangea on the wall of our house.

The tape was left tangled in the branches long after the nest had disappeared.

John Graham
Beckermet, Cumberland

SIR – We have to live with our back door open, on account of the swallows nesting in the loft.

They come and go by the minute, zooming in at full speed and banking sharply up the stairwell with miraculous precision. They take little notice of us, even as we stand in the open doorway.

Dick Park
Bridport, Dorset

SIR — In early spring I brought some sheep's wool home from the fields and scattered it around my garden for birds to use as nesting material.

The crows took some of the wool and dunked it in the garden pond. I assume they did this to remove the fatty lanolin from the wool, as it turned from light grey to white after a few days of soaking. They then laid it in strips to dry in the sun before taking it to their nest.

George Sullivan
Cubbington, Warwickshire

SIR — On my allotment sparrows help themselves to the twine I use to tie my runner-bean canes together. But I don't bear them a grudge: on finding one chap caught up in the netting over my brassicas, I spent quite some time cutting him out, thus enabling him to raid my garden again.

Colin Brown
Castor, Northamptonshire

SIR – Sparrows have pinched so many bits from the lining of my hanging basket that the bare minimum remains to contain the compost. Then they teach their young to 'bathe' in the dry soil of the flower beds, throwing it all over the path.

Still, I enjoy having them visit the garden, so continue to feed them.

Sheila Weary
Evesham, Worcestershire

SIR – Every year, to ensure that nesting birds are not disturbed, my wife bans grandchildren, dogs and myself from sections of the garden.

This year's no-go areas were my shed (a robin nesting in an artificial Christmas tree), the vegetable patch (blackbird in the hedge) and the front of the house (a ring-necked dove sitting on an egg in a hanging basket).

William McWilliams
Kingsnorth, Kent

SIR – The last time I tried to clean out our nesting box, my fingers met with a nest of warm baby mice.

John Goulding
Potters Bar, Hertfordshire

BATS IN THE BELFRY

SIR – Your correspondent is being rather disingenuous when she says the majority of churches live happily with their bats.

At Holy Trinity Church, Tattershall, we are 'lucky' to have between 600 and 1,000 bats roosting in the church. It costs us approximately £1,000 a year for plastic sheeting and cleaning materials. To be in the church late on a summer evening is like being in a nature programme.

Doug Eke
Tattershall, Lincolnshire

SIR – There is an easy solution for the clergyman who complained about badgers on church property and bats in his belfry.

He only has to baptise, confirm and marry them, and he will never see them again.

Jane Kelly
London W3

PEACOCK MATCHMAKING

SIR – Perhaps the residents of Breadsall, Derbyshire, who are 'spitting feathers over a mischievous peacock', could have a word with Kevin and tell him about Henny-Penny, a lonely peahen who turned up here last year.

She roosts in a tree, has breakfast and tea with our hens, loves spaghetti and white bread and spends hours looking at herself in the windows.

Camilla Borradaile
Blandford Forum, Dorset

SIR – Our village has also had a fly-in peacock, Charlie, for the last year. He is extremely decorative, but also very loud. His positive visual qualities, however, are negated by his effect on flower beds which he destroys, taking the early flowers as they appear.

Recently, things have been complicated further by a fly-in peahen, who is even noisier, and sounds like a rusty donkey.

Is this happening up and down the country?

Robert Kirby
Maer, Staffordshire

SIR — In the late 1990s I worked at the Institute of Orthopaedics at the Royal National Orthopaedic Hospital in Stanmore. Percy the peacock was an ever-present car park attendant, frequently blocking the entrance to the offices.

To divert his vigilant behaviour, two peahens were purchased in the hope that he would be distracted. Two weeks later he threw himself in front of an oncoming car and was killed.

Karen Pollak
Watford, Hertfordshire

SIR — I taught the reception class at a Hertfordshire primary school for 20 years, and for about six or seven of those years we had a resident peacock who was expelled from the local manor by the peahens.

In the morning, having slept on the roof or in one of the trees in the school field or adjoining churchyard, he waited outside the kitchen for the cook to arrive, as she fed him a daily snack. He spent the day parading around, displaying his tail.

He was a joy and delight to us all; and although he was a bit noisy at times, he was no worse than the children.

Ruth E. Banks
Pelham, Hertfordshire

COCK A DOODLE NOO

SIR – You report the case of a cockerel threatened with execution because it crows too early in the morning. There is a simple cure. A cockerel needs to stand up to his full height in order to stretch his neck to crow.

The answer is to keep him in a coop with a low roof, or with some chicken wire stretched across, so that he cannot stand up fully. If he is let out at a reasonable hour, he will then stretch and crow. He will be happy, and so will the intolerant neighbours.

Joan Bridgman
Littleton, Somerset

GRANDFATHER WAS QUITE A CATCH

SIR — My grandfather was out with a girl in Richmond Park, where there were swallows flying overhead. He reached up as if to catch one and actually did. When asked what he was going to do with it, he promptly replied: 'Oh, I usually let them go.'

Nick Cutts
Yelverton, Devon

SIR — One August on a Yorkshire moor, a single grouse flew straight down the line of butts. Guns stayed lowered, but in the end butt Major General Sir Brian Wyldbore-Smith, height 6ft 2in, stood up, held out his cap and caught it.

Lady Mather
Macclesfield, Cheshire

SIR – I, too, witnessed a slightly bizarre catch while supervising a game of primary-school rounders. The ball caught the top edge of the bat and went spinning directly upwards, instantly killing a small bird which was flying above. Seeing an object falling towards her, the backstop ran forward to catch it. A soft dead bird and not a tennis ball landed in her outstretched hands.

David Davies
Newburgh, Lancashire

SIR – Over the weekend, I was sitting on the terrace opening a bottle of champagne. The cork went off with a great report, and this morning I discovered a dead pigeon lying close to the cork on the pavement across the road. Can I claim a first for this method of pigeon shooting?

John Francis
Ludlow, Shropshire

SIR — Humans aren't the only ones to make unusual catches. Our old and sick cat was one day sitting on top of the television, when a robin flew into the room. She opened her mouth and the bird flew straight in. It had been many years since she'd had the agility to catch her own prey and she looked pleased with herself, although somewhat bemused.

Gwyn Evans
Whitland, Carmarthenshire

KEEPING UP WITH THE AMINS

SIR — Your obituary of Lt Gen Sir Chandos Blair did not mention one crucial incident in the 'Denis Hills affair' which, I believe, ensured that the British teacher and writer was not executed.

Idi Amin, who was my erstwhile platoon commander in 4 King's African Rifles, knew that I kept and bred a number of exotic birds at my home in East Anglia. On one of my previous visits to Uganda, he had bemoaned the fact that the leaders of Zaire and Kenya had managed to acquire pure white peafowl. 'Here, in Uganda,' he said, 'I have only blue ones.'

When he asked if I could help, I thought for a while before replying: 'Labda' (maybe) and giving him a stern look, the meaning of which was not lost on him.

Shortly before Chan Blair and I left Uganda, I was able to have a final quiet word with the president. He still wanted the white peafowl.

'Well, first you must ensure Mr Hills returns safely to England,' I replied.

Amin grinned and nodded.

Amin got his pair of white peafowl and, several years later, they were still thriving in Entebbe Zoo.

Major Iain Grahame
Bures, Suffolk

ANCIENT MARINERS

SIR – Coming off evening watch while in the merchant navy many years ago, I went aloft to sit on the aft-hatch and sample a breath of fresh air. Seated immediately beside me every evening was a grey-headed albatross, tall and stately, the wind ruffling his tail feathers. After a single glance in my direction, he resumed gazing forward at the rising moon.

Eight or nine days out of New Zealand, as we approached Pitcairn Island, this great bird disappeared as usual as daylight came, but failed to reappear again with nightfall.

Is it possible that these wonderful creatures, credited with epic migratory feats, sometimes cheat by cadging lifts in this way?

Peter Foley
Ilford, Essex

SIR — The dignity of the albatross is not always its strength. While I was crossing the Pacific on a large bulk carrier some years ago, I noticed that the hatch tops had become courting grounds for wandering albatrosses. One large male, displaying proudly to assembled admirers, toppled backwards from hatch to deck and became trapped between the hatches and pipe-runs.

The chief and second officers built a makeshift bridge over the pipes and tried to shoo the Lothario to safety. The bird turned, spread its wings and offered a huge gaping beak. Both men executed an astonishing 5ft standing leap and scrambled to safety.

In its own good time, the albatross found its way over the bridge and stalked haughtily away, dignity somewhat restored.

Captain Ross
Jolliffe, Norwich

SIR – Finding owls, herons and even bats on North Sea oil rigs is nothing new. When I worked on an exploration rig midway between Shetland and Norway in the Seventies we had many such visitors.

One time in 1976, thick fog forced an owl to take refuge at the end of one of our rig's flare booms. We managed to grab the owl and put it in a big box in the warm to dry out, feeding it slivers of raw pork.

Taking one of the supply boats back to Shetland, I brought the owl with me. The boat skipper was concerned about the implications of bringing live animals to shore and asked me to release the owl before we made harbour. I opened the box on deck and the bird jumped out on to the railings. It waited a few minutes, looked back at me and then unfolded an enormous wingspan and flew off towards land.

Roger Oliver
Kingston upon Thames, Surrey

PIGEON NAV

SIR — Professor Guilford is off course in reaching his conclusion that pigeons navigate by following roads. Pigeons, like other birds, follow roads because the updraught from the heat generated by motor vehicles makes for easier flying: ask any glider pilot.

C.J. Lord
Heswall, Wirral

SIR — While returning from an anti-submarine patrol in 1943, we had to crash-land our Whitley on a little harbourless island called Foula just west of the Shetland islands. I let go two pigeons with SOS messages attached. My SOS before we crash-landed had also been picked up.

We were found by a lifeboat and embarked on a three-day journey to get back to RAF Wick, 100 or so miles away. The first thing we did was ask if the pigeons had got back. One day later our feathered friends flew in, virtually to a military band.

A Met man told us that the birds would not negotiate the cold front lying between Foula and Wick, and would have flown round it, via Holland.

No motorways or roads to aid them, just oceans of North Sea. Clever little birds.

Eric Harrison
Cheadle, Staffordshire

SIR — You report that hundreds of racing pigeons have vanished in the 'Bermuda triangle of the North of England'. In the past, pigeon fanciers have blamed birds of prey or the army of moggies that patrol our country.

However, there may be a simpler explanation: faced with a life of hard labour, these birds may have chosen a life of easy pickings and little work.

In bored moments at railway stations, I have counted the number of birds that have rings on their legs; around 10 per cent of the larger group of pigeons are former racing or homing pigeons that have gone feral.

Ray Harrington-Vail
Newport, Isle of Wight

SIR — Regarding reports of racing pigeons being lost from the Queen's loft at Sandringham, Her Majesty may wish to be aware that, during winter monitoring of pigeon prey at the eyries of peregrine falcons, rings belonging to her birds are found occasionally.

I carry on my key-ring the ring of one such racing pigeon, ringed in 2001, bearing the code ER 062.

Bill Trobe
Newcastle upon Tyne

SIR — I had a similar experience to your correspondent who travelled with a pigeon on the Tube. I was en route to Baker Street on the Metropolitan line when a pigeon got on at Finchley Road. It stood facing the door until we both alighted at Baker Street. My last sight of it was when it strutted purposefully towards the escalator to the Bakerloo line, presumably on the way to Trafalgar Square.

Jack Wintle
Ruislip, Middlesex

'WAIT! That's my luggage'

HOBBY HORSES

MOUNTED PARLIAMENTARIANS

SIR — James Gray is not the first MP to ride into the Palace of Westminster since 1920, although I commend his reason for doing so, since I am also implacably opposed to the export of live horses for slaughter. I rode to Parliament on a thoroughbred in 1996 to deliver a petition calling for fair rates for riding schools.

There are still tethering rings at the palace, and the arches within are built for horse-drawn carriages. It is a pity that more MPs do not commute on horseback.

Harry Greenway
MP for Ealing North, 1979–97
London SW1

DRUNK IN CHARGE OF A RIDER

SIR — We may have found the answer to how to get to a rural pub: we ride our horses, on the assumption that as we amble homewards, it is the horses that are in charge of us.

The only drawback is that the horses themselves are quite partial to a slurp of cider, raising the question of who is drunk in charge of whom.

Juliet Johns
Carnon Downs, Cornwall

SIR — Those who ride a horse after drinking need to be careful. There is an offence under the 1872 Licensing Act of being drunk in charge of a horse. I imagine that the defence of the horse being in charge will do little good.

Don't try a horse and carriage: the same applies and, if someone is injured, there is the risk of being charged with wanton and furious driving under the Offences Against the Person Act, 1861. This also covers bicycles and steam engines.

Alan Kibblewhite
Blandford, Dorset

SIR — Recently, while driving into Sheffield, I came across a magnificently dressed horseman, on top of an equally splendid horse, on the public highway. Nothing wrong with that, but the gentleman was speaking into a mobile telephone. Is this a traffic violation?

Derek Harrison
Bakewell, Derbyshire

SIR — The highway code for leisurely Cyprus in the 1960s contained this warning: 'Do not fall asleep upon your cart. To do so is a danger to yourself and to other road users.'

Robert Stephenson
Henley-on-Thames, Oxon

SIR — Lying in a field soaking up the sun last week, my wife and I were politely asked by approaching horseriders if we would mind standing up and talking. Otherwise, they said, their mounts would not pass, thinking we were dead.

John Goulding
Potters Bar, Hertfordshire

SIR – One of the more unusual rural signs must be the one, near Chorley, which advertised 'last horse manure before the M6'.

Alan Barker
Accrington, Lancashire

PAMPERED PONIES

SIR – The other day my daughter asked me why it was that, although dog owners are now expected to clean up after their animals, the same does not seem to apply to horse owners. As we stepped around another large, steaming pile, I found myself stumped for an answer.

Anne Carrington
Bridgeyate, Gloucestershire

SIR – All horses in Bruges wear nappies.

Peter de Snoo
Truro, Cornwall

SIR — Your correspondent who proposes nappies for horses should make the most of the free manure.

In Cornwall as a small child I would watch with horror as my father rushed out, shovelled up steaming deposits from passing horses and dumped them on the rhubarb — which I was later forced to eat. It was, however, declicious.

Jill Bayly
Salisbury, Wiltshire

SIR — I am reminded of a story about an inmate peering over the wall of an asylum and asking a gardener why he is collecting horse manure.

When the gardener says it's to put on his rhubarb, the inmate responds that he should join them in the asylum as they have custard on theirs.

Clive Robinson
Old Glossop, Derbyshire

SIR — I once lived on a country lane shared by cows on their way to being milked. As a result, my white car was usually splattered with cow dung. When the company for whom I worked decided that I deserved a car upgrade, I asked the salesman if they had one in Cow Muck Khaki.

His reply: 'Yes, we do, sir, but we call it Harvest Gold.'

Michael Tod
Abergavenny, Monmouthshire

FOUR LEGS VS FOUR WHEELS

SIR — It has always seemed to me to be a little illogical that you have to be 16 years old in order to ride a motorcycle on the road when that bike can only go in one direction, yet you can ride a horse or pony on the road at any age and that animal can go forwards, backwards, sideways or upwards. I have seen children as young as five or six mounted on an animal that they cannot possibly have the strength or skill to control.

There should be a minimum age (say 16) before a rider can take a horse on the road and then only after taking a test.

Peter Williams
Newbury, Berkshire

SIR — I do not know any horse riders who like going on the road, thanks to the lack of care and attention from cars, vans, motorcycles and buses. Most are forced to use the road in order to gain access to one of the few bridle paths left.

Support horse riders in their struggle to open up more bridleways, and you won't see us for dust.

Jane Brittain-Long
Newnham on Severn, Gloucestershire

SIR — The excellent way drivers behave around horses and their riders never ceases to amaze me. Is their reduced speed and wide berth anything to do with the fact that horse riders almost always give drivers an enthusiastic wave of gratitude?

I hardly ever get the same reaction from a cyclist. Perhaps if cyclists were to adopt the same tactic, they too would enjoy safe passage.

Tom Kean
Blount, Oxfordshire

SIR — It is evident that some of your readers have but one priority when driving — that is, to complete their journey quickly, and to hell with anything that gets in the way.

My attitude is rather different. I acknowledge the ancient rights of pedestrians, dogs, cats, and birds, to name a few.

HOBBY HORSES

I love to see horses out and about — two abreast or not. To me, they represent treasured evidence that there is still an old England out there, with generally prudent and polite people perpetuating a national tradition.

Bill Franklin
Haywards Heath, West Sussex

SIR — How immeasurably more romantic it was when the Duchess of Cambridge left the Abbey with her new husband in a horse-drawn carriage, instead of the car in which she had arrived. The cavalry escort also looked splendid in the hazy sunshine.

We are a people identified with the horse, from the prehistoric chalk horses on our hills to the pony clubs that our daughters love to join. Horses are no longer the mainstay of the plough, but, by golly, they are the centre of a most democratic interest, from Duke to dustman, on the racecourse.

Henrietta Harris
Reading, Berkshire

THE HOOVES OF THE BASKERVILLES

SIR — It is possible that the Romanian cattle rustlers who disguised the tracks of two stolen çows by fitting them with Wellington boots are fans of Sherlock Holmes.

The report bears a strong resemblance to the case of *The Adventure of the Priory School*, where the villain shod horses with shoes that resembled cows' tracks, to confuse pursuers.

Daron Gunson
Bures, Essex

WARRIOR HORSE

SIR — Your report about the film of *War Horse* reminded me of a talk by Brough Scott about his grandfather, Jack Seely, and his horse Warrior.

Seely and Warrior arrived in France in August 1914. They survived some of the worst battles, including Passchendaele, and led the last great cavalry charge of 1,000 horses of the Canadian Cavalry in March 1918.

According to legend, Seely recommended Warrior be given a Victoria Cross with the citation: 'He went everywhere I went'.

Warrior had a good retirement and died aged 32.

Denise Bowker
Ringmer, Hampshire

PRICELESS PIT PONY

SIR — Pit ponies suffered a lot, as your correspondent points out, but they also saved miners' lives. My father was a miner at Marley Hill. Once, his pit pony would not move forwards or backwards. Just then, there were two roof falls, one behind him and one in front. Had it not been for the pony, I would not have a father. My father gave the pony all his sandwiches for the day.

David Burgess
Thurmaston, Leicestershire

SIR — It was no surprise to me to read the report that a horse can find its way home. As a child, I helped a farmer on his milk-round by horse and float. We never forgot to deliver anyone's daily milk: the pony knew the route infallibly, so he stopped at all the right places, knew how long it should take to deliver the pints and would move on, all without a command.

John Wain
Torquay, Devon

LIVE ANOTHER DAY

SIR — Madonna, who has broken her collarbone while riding, should get straight back on the horse. My father, Darby Haddon, broke his while hunting with the Heythrop. He continued hunting, jumping the Cotswold stone walls, with his arm in a sling, holding his reins with the left hand.

At the age of 73 he fell off and knocked himself unconscious while hunting on Exmoor. He came to when he was on a gate being transported to the nearest road. He insisted on being driven home rather than going to hospital.

Probably his most dangerous brush with death came when he cut his leg and it would not heal. He treated it with horse liniment, then split a drainpipe, covered his leg with it, and continued hunting for several days. Only when the leg started to turn black did he reluctantly seek medical treatment.

I miss him.

Celia Haddon
London SW1

CREEPY,
FLYING CRAWLIES

'I don't mind the midges,
but we're plagued by
Westminster politicians'

ROTTEN MIDGE DETERRENTS

SIR – Some years ago I was in a pub in a remote part of the Scottish Highlands. One of the locals told me that the best midge deterrent was brown sugar, rubbed all over one's face.

'It stops them biting, does it?' I asked.

With guffaws from his pals he replied: 'No, but it rots their teeth.'

Ray Byrne
Cheadle Hulme, Cheshire

SIR – I can recommend taking up tobacco smoking. Midges hate it. Even when not actually smoking, a smoker has enough nicotine in his blood to discourage the beasts. It is no accident that tobacco smoking is more prevalent in Scotland than in any other part of Britain.

Michael Phillips
Olney, Buckinghamshire

SIR – I've lived on the west coast of Scotland for some 30 years. In an effort to avoid the dreaded midge, I have tried all possible deterrents and have discovered the only effective method is to move away.

Roger Hatcher
Garelochhead, Dunbartonshire

SIR – The Highland midge has made a great mistake migrating south, as you report. When they become an English problem and not just a Scottish one, we can be sure that the entire arsenal and treasury of the Westminster Government will be focused on their eradication.

Dr Eamonn Butler
London SW1

SIR – None of the various chironomid or nemocerous insects known loosely as midges has an air speed of more than about 5mph. They are troublesome only in more-or-less windless conditions and are outpaced by the most leisurely cyclist.

However, I can offer your correspondent little comfort if Buckinghamshire has been invaded by the dreaded Highland strain, of which Para Handy tells us, 'They'll bite their way through corrugated iron roofs to get at ye.'

Robin Dow
Stocksbridge, South Yorkshire

DUNG BEETLE SAFARI

SIR — I agree with James Kirkup's article: 'Forget big cat sightings — an angry badger is magic to me'.

My family and I once joined a dawn game walk at Victoria Falls. Having grown up in Zimbabwe we were perhaps rather too used to seeing larger, more 'dangerous' animals. However, on this occasion, there was not a single large animal to be seen — not even an antelope.

Our intrepid guide wasn't in the least fazed: we were treated to a fascinating talk about dung beetles. I had no idea that there were so many types, or what they got up to.

It has stayed in my memory as one of the most interesting game walks I've ever experienced.

Ali Kirwin
Dunkeswell, Devon

SOCK, SANDALS AND SEPTICAEMIA

SIR — I recently yielded to the wave of public opinion against the sock and sandal combination and mowed the lawn in sockless sandals. Big mistake.

A few days later, I was overcome with a migraine, high temperature, shivering and a red leg. Within hours, I was hooked up to saline and antibiotic drips, and spent a long weekend in hospital recovering from advanced cellulitis (with the prospect of septicaemia), a condition that kills 1,000 people a year. All this because some insect enjoys nibbling a tasty foot or ankle.

I shall, in future, abandon all attempts at sartorial elegance (I am, after all, over 37) and on every possible occasion wear my socks — probably blue, a colour apparently offensive to flying insects — regardless of my neighbours' tutting.

Jeremy Burton
Shurlock Row, Berkshire

SIR — Your correspondent notes that his blue-painted study is fly-less but full of spiders. I wonder whether there is a connection.

Gerard Parke-Hatton
Preston, Lancashire

NO FLY ZONE

SIR — There was a time when children asked me: 'Where do flies go in the winter time?'

Not any more. Last summer, we rarely saw a house-fly. Now, in January, they are everywhere in our house. Armed with rolled-up *Daily Telegraphs*, we have declared total war.

Is this unprecedented invasion the result of global warming, perhaps auguring a nightmare scenario to rival Hitchcock's *The Birds*?

John Cottrell
Addlestone, Surrey

CREEPY, FLYING CRAWLIES

SIR – I wish to disagree with your correspondent who suggests a rolled-up copy of *The Daily Telegraph* as a fly swat. A solid object such as a rolled-up newspaper creates a bow-wave of air in front of itself. This displaced air reaches the fly a split second ahead of the paper, thus adding additional impetus to the fly's take-off speed.

A conventional fly-swat, however, by virtue of its permeability, creates no bow-wave and has a much better chance of a hit.

One should also take into account the fact that the initial movement of a fly on take-off is backwards. To angle one's swipe accordingly gives an even better chance of a hit. I have often caught a fly in my hand by a sudden swift grab from behind.

Geoffrey R. Rowson
Taunton, Somerset

SIR — For the aficionado of wasp shooting, may I recommend the Berloque Pistole loaded with a 78rpm gramophone needle. Still available today, this unique miniature pistol makes short work of wasps at distances of up to six feet.

Paul Hargreaves
East Grinstead, West Sussex

DISCERNING BEES

SIR — A rogue swarm of honey bees has arrived in our garden, and we are now going to integrate it into one of our smaller colonies. The way to do this is to put a layer of paper between the new swarm and the old. By the time the new swarm eats through the paper the two swarms should be used to each other.

When I asked my husband what paper we should use, he said: 'They like *The Daily Telegraph*.' Apparently it is something to do with the paper and ink used.

Amanda Gavin
Reading, Berkshire

SIR – A customer once demanded to know if my honey was organic. I told him that bees make about 40,000 journeys per year, anywhere within a three-mile radius of their hive. Did he think anyone was going to follow them to find out where they collected the nectar?

David Green
Castle Morris, Pembrokeshire

LADYBIRD MANSION

SIR – I was recently given a beautifully made ladybird house for my birthday. The instructions inside say: 'The size of the hole in this ladybird box makes it suitable for ladybirds up to the size of a sparrow or nuthatch.'

It is made in China, for Sainsbury's, and there is a 'careline' for comments. I am at a loss to know what comment to make.

Mick Crook
Little Haywood, Staffordshire

STICKING IT TO THE DEVIL ANTS

SIR — Regarding 'super ants', we had many years' experience of the little devils when we lived in Greece.

These fire ants got everywhere, and particularly into electrical appliances and sockets. Many an evening was spent with no lights due to their chewing through power cables in the walls.

The only sure-fire way of defeating them was Blu-Tac; a thin layer spread around the edges of a socket seemed to keep them at bay.

I found it difficult to keep them out of some appliances though, such as the sewing machine or computer.

Alan Jones
Boston, Lincolnshire

SIR — As a student I spent a long vacation in Pokhara, Nepal. My hosts thwarted ants by placing each leg of furniture in a small bowl of water.

Anne Atkins
Horspath, Oxfordshire

CREEPY, FLYING CRAWLIES

SIR – When I lived on a farm in Argentina, armies of ants marched through our house.

Having tried the usual poisons with no luck, I took local advice and buried a calf's liver two feet deep and two feet from the house. It worked like magic.

Carol Thwaites
London SW15

SIR – What about an aardvark?

Tim Peachey
Ross-on-Wye, Herefordshire

SIR – The benefit of an aardvark to control domestic ants is more than offset by the problem of clearing up after the aardvark.

P. J. Reardon
Tonbridge, Kent

SIR – I have found a collection of strategically placed 2p coins to be an excellent and permanent ant-banisher.

Carol Harlow
Guildford, Surrey

SNAIL TRAIL

SIR — What gets into snails? Our metal garden table has a trail showing that an intrepid snail has scaled its fretworked heights, circumnavigating the top before descending again.

We also have a snail trail across our upstairs bedroom window. What are these little explorers searching for?

Hugh Bebb
Sunbury-on-Thames, Middlesex

SIR — Why do snails climb walls? Because they're there, of course.

Tim Nixon
Braunton, Devon

SIR — We mulch the veg patch with rotted horse manure that is rich in brandling worms. When it rains heavily, the worms cross the garden path and climb the house wall. We have seen them as high as 20ft off the ground and we have to assume that they only stop when they reach the eaves.

We have never seen them come back down; do they parachute at night?

R. Allan Reese
Forston, Dorset

CREEPY, FLYING CRAWLIES

SIR – Following your report on getting rid of snails, I have employed the fast bowler of our local cricket team to instruct my wife in the art of the 'full toss'. My neighbours, though, are using the same ploy, so it's more like tennis than cricket.

David J. Hartshorn
Daventry, Northamptonshire

SIR – My slug count has now exceeded 1,000. Rather than attracting them with cat food, I use beer – which initially did the trick, but now, by torchlight, I see them curled over the rim, drinking the beer but not falling in.

Dorothy Foreman
Burton-upon-Stather, Lincolnshire

SIR – I have a No 1 haircut which is refreshed weekly by my partner.

The fine short clippings are brushed up and sprinkled in our garden containers, which works wonders in keeping away the slugs. However, big as my head is, my hair follicles cannot produce enough to cover the entire garden.

Is there an opportunity here for hairdressers to increase income and recycle at the same time?

Patrick Tracey
Carlisle, Cumbria

SIR — Now that my throwing of unwanted garden snails has been curtailed by arthritis, I am considering making a scaled-down medieval Trebuchet. Searching in our barn for suitable materials I came across an old clay pigeon trap. Trials last evening, witnessed by my dog, have proved most effective, with considerable distances achieved.

This method may not be practical for town dwellers. So for those living on the South Coast, could I suggest putting unwanted English snails in strawberry punnets attached to balloons? A brisk prevailing wind should achieve a speedy Channel crossing, possibly sparking off competitive snail flying races and, at the same time, feeding any itinerant hungry Frenchman.

Paul Spencer Schofield
Harewood, West Yorkshire

'I'm trying to throw it into next door's garden'

P.S.

P.S.

A DOG'S BEST FRIEND

SIR — On one of our regular walks in Norfolk, we pass a solitary goat in a small paddock. On one occasion, there was a chicken strutting around in the enclosure with him.

I stroked the goat as usual and offered him some fresh grass, but, as I left, the chicken flew at me, pecking at my legs. I shooed it away three times before it quit its assault. Obviously, it saw itself as the goat's friend.

I learnt later that their owner went into the paddock with her dog, which attacked and killed the chicken, at which point the goat had attacked the dog.

The dog survived, but the goat pined for two weeks: he wouldn't go into his shelter where he and the chicken used to sleep.

It seems beyond belief that such an affection could develop between these two creatures, but we all need companionship and animals are no exception.

Ann Beeton
Goffs Oak, Hertfordshire

SIR — Ann Beeton's letter reminded me that on my father's dairy farm we had a goose that left its flock to become a companion to a cow.

The goose would browse in the field alongside the cow during the day, and would accompany its friend into the shippen at milking time.

Janet Bobbett
Kendal, Westmorland

SIR — I read with interest about the use of aggressive llamas for guarding farm property. Llamas are, in fact, very peaceful animals and, unless badly handled, pose little risk to people.

While llamas are used as guards, this is usually for sheep and chickens against marauding foxes and dogs. The llama will bond with the sheep and become the flock leader. It can pack quite a punch and will charge a fox and try to knock it over.

I heard of a sad case recently where a llama had been guarding sheep for some years. Eventually things changed on the farm and the sheep were sold off. The llama was so distraught at losing his flock that he simply pined away.

Tim Crowfoot
Southampton, Hampshire

SIR — My late husband, a shepherd for more than 25 years, always said that from the moment a lamb was born, it spent the rest of its life thinking of ways to die, preferably by a method that no other sheep had tried. He devoted his life to trying to be one step ahead.

Ilse Eve
Gallowstree Common, Oxfordshire